JAN 7 1987		
JAN 2 5 1987		
AUG 2 4 1988		
OCT 1 1 2001		

FINANCE FOR MINE MANAGEMENT

FINANCE FOR
MINE MANAGEMENT

R. M. WANLESS, FCA
Partner, Coopers & Lybrand

 METHUEN
TORONTO, SYDNEY, AUCKLAND

First published in 1983 by
Chapman and Hall Ltd
11 New Fetter Lane
London EC4P 4EE

Published in Canada by Methuen Publications
2330 Midland Avenue, Agincourt, Ontario M1S 1P7

Canadian Cataloguing in Publication Data

Wanless, Roderick M., 1935–
    Finance for mine management

Includes index.
ISBN 0-458-95640-6

1. Mining industry and finance.   2. Mine management.   1. Title.
TN274.W35   622'.068'1   C82-094663-X

Now to the future cast your eyes,
For there, aye there, the challenge lies.
Unknown, unseen, untested yet,
But promise-filled for those who set
Their sights beyond some simple role
And seek a more demanding goal —
Find ore! More ore! And yet more still! —
Then face the task with iron will.

Selwyn B. Jones

CONTENTS

ACKNOWLEDGEMENTS

I am greatly indebted to my partners in Coopers & Lybrand, and my associates and friends who assisted me in so many ways in the writing of this book. Particular acknowledgements are due to J.P. Fairchild (audit partner) and J.R. Hay (tax manager), both of our Vancouver office, for their assistance to me in writing Chapters 5 and 7. My sincere thanks to B.J.L. Rolfe of Leslie, Wright & Rolfe, Ltd, a Vancouver insurance firm, for assistance in the insurance section in Chapter 8; to George Stevens of Lawrence & Shaw, a Vancouver law firm, for his advice on portions of Chapter 1; and to R.E. Hallbauer, Vice-President Mining, Teck Corporation, Vancouver, for all his constructive comments and criticisms. Last, but not least, I thank my wife, Do, without whose patience and understanding both my enthusiasm and manuscripts would have long since found their way to the waste dump.

R.M. Wanless

INTRODUCTION

At the beginning of any project there should be a clearly defined objective in view. This book and its companion publication *Mine Management* indicate the very broad range of subjects to be covered relating to the management of a mining operation.

This book in particular was conceived and written for a specific purpose and with a particular range of reader in mind. The topics covered deal with corporate structures and financial matters as they relate to the broad spectrum of activities within a mining company. It is presumed that those with a financial background will be aware of the concepts and principles covered. For this reason the discussion of topics is primarily directed to those members, or aspiring members, of the management team who do not have a financial background. I hope that the book will provide an appropriate level of insight into the corporations and other structures within which mining companies operate and the financial matters which are an integral part of managing every mining organization.

The topics are discussed at various levels, some in a broad sense, others in detail, to provide the financial background required by members of the mine management team to carry out their duties more effectively.

The topics are covered in a logical sequence beginning with a description of corporate and other organizational structures. From this point the financial considerations flow from the finding of a mine to the feasibility study, plant construction and operation, and related matters such as shareholders' financial statements, taxation and aspects of corporate financial security.

In order to put the various stages from location to production in perspective and to show the integration and overlap of key functions the following chart is appropriate:

The birth of a mine

Function	1	2	3	4	5	6	7	8	9	10	11	12	13	14	15	16	17	18	19	20
Location and acquisition	—																			
Exploration		—	—																	
Feasibility			—	—																
Engineering and design					—	—	—	—	—	—	—	—	—	—	—	—	—	—		
Sales contract				—	—	—														
Financing				—	—	—	—													
Development					—	—	—	—	—	—	—	—	—	—	—	—	—	—		
Construction							—	—	—	—	—	—	—	—	—	—	—	—	—	
Tune-up																		—	—	
Production																			—	—

A knowledge of the financial aspects of these functions, even on a general basis, must be considered a tool of management. In this book I attempt to describe these tools and how they may be used.

INDEX TO THE APPENDIX (PAGE 185)

The Appendix is not intended to include all aspects of management reports but represents merely a cross-section of some management information gathering and reporting methods. It provides the reader with an opportunity to see what some reports look like and what detail they contain. The following samples are included in the Appendix.

- Sample general ledger code of accounts for use during preproduction and construction (underground operation)
- Sample feasibility cash flow forecast; project break-even calculation: metal price $1.90/lb
- Sample feasibility cash flow forecast: metal price $2.40/lb
- Sample feasibility cash flow forecast: metal price $2.75/lb
- Operations cost summary (sample for an open pit operation)
- Mill operating cost summary (sample report to support amount shown on operations cost summary, Table A.4)

- Cost centre summary – 23 Grinding (sample report to support amount shown on mill operating cost summary, Table A.5)
- Cost centre detail – 23 Grinding (sample report to show cost centre detail in different form to support cost centre summary, Table A.6)

CORPORATIONS AND OTHER ORGANIZATIONAL STRUCTURES

Out of the ever-present social revolution has come an awareness of personal and group rights resulting in a greater influence of government over business. It is imperative that a mine manager understand the type of organization within which his business operates. These organizations range from corporations to joint ventures, partnerships of various types and proprietorships. Each organization has its own specific advantages and disadvantages which depend on the requirements and objectives of management. The organizational vehicle to be used may vary depending on the size and stage of the mining project, the money involved, the complexities of financing, the co-ordination and relationship with other business, the extent of international involvement and the extent of public participation. Government legislation in many parts of the world may not allow management the most desired latitude in the selection of an operating vehicle. It is important, however, that management should have a reasonable working knowledge of the general, operational, organizational and legal concepts of the most common business vehicles in order to achieve the maximum results and to discharge properly the ever-increasing onus of management responsibility.

The mining industry is very capital intensive with more than its fair share of relative risk. A corporation, as discussed in greater detail later, limits the liability of the shareholder and facilitates the raising of capital via the medium of public issues of capital stock (shares). It is for this reason that virtually all mining ventures are carried on within the organizational structure known as a limited liability stock company, and commonly called a limited company or a corporation. Even though many major projects are financed through long-term debt, the lenders usually insist on a substantial equity investment which means risk capital, often raised from a large number of stockholders.

Corporate structures, joint ventures and other business organizations are basically the same in every industry. There is little within the concepts to require any significant difference for a mining company. Mine management also have the same responsibilities as management in any other industry, and it is therefore necessary that their level of knowledge be at least adequate.

This chapter is meant to provide mine management with an overview of some of the most common organizational vehicles, their basic structure and particular uses together with some of the more pertinent responsibilities relating to them. A summary of the points to be covered includes:

- Corporations, divisions, subsidiaries and effectively controlled corporations
- Joint ventures
- Proprietorships and partnerships
- A new private mining company
- The public company

CORPORATIONS

Basic concept

A corporation is a separate legal entity which may be created by a person or group of people through the incorporation process as stipulated by the applicable law, usually a Companies Act, in the jurisdiction of incorporation. A corporation has the rights, powers, duties, and obligations as governed by its own incorporating documents or the incorporating Act and must abide by all other legislation relative to the jurisdiction(s) in which it is incorporated or operates. In most countries a corporation may sue and be sued.

Corporation ownership is governed by the ownership of its issued shares. Control may be secured by ownership of more than 50% of the issued voting shares of capital stock. In many instances effective control can be achieved through the holding of less than 50% provided management can solicit sufficient voting support or proxies from other shareholders. In the accounting sense, significant influence is considered to exist when ownership is between 20% and 50%.

A shareholder in a corporation is limited in his liability to that corporation or its creditors to the amount which he pays or agrees to pay to the corporation for his share. Some exceptions to this rule exist in circumstances where the amount paid or payable is less than the par value of the issued shares.

At the time a company is incorporated the incorporator will determine the classes and number of shares of each class that the corporation will be authorized to issue. The two main classes of share capital are common shares and preferred shares with the preferred shares having such rights and restrictions as provided at the time of or subsequent to their creation. Preferred shares usually do not have the right to vote but rank before the common shares in distributions on liquidation, bankruptcy and usually in receipt of dividends. Common shares usually have the right of one vote for each share owned. Various classes of common shares ('A' and 'B' common) have become increasingly popular, particularly where it is desirable to retain voting control but allow a different ownership or equity ratio. In a case such as this, one class of common shares would be given one vote per share with the other class having two or more votes per share, while both classes rank equally in equity and in dividends.

Most countries or jurisdictions of incorporation provide that a corporation may be private (non-reporting) or public (reporting) with a variety of definitions and rules relative to each particular category. It is natural to expect more stringent corporate and securities legislation to apply in the case of a public company with appropriate transitional provisions when a private company becomes a public company. It should be noted that in most circumstances a private company is restricted in the number of its shareholders and the transfer of shares, and is prohibited from asking the public at large to subscribe to its shares. A public company may sell its shares to the public only after complying with the applicable securities legislation which normally would require the prior issuance of a prospectus or similar document. A public company will be listed on a stock exchange only on acceptance of a listing application and compliance with such other requirements as the applicable securities commission and/or listing exchange may require.

Operational concept

The corporation is the most common vehicle used for the conduct of business, and the concept of the corporation is the same throughout the world. The primary advantages of the corporate entity are subject to securities legislation but basically include:

1. The ease of division and identification of ownership by means of shares
2. Limitation of liability of the shareholder
3. Marketability and liquidity of the shares of a public company listed on a stock exchange
4. The ability of the corporation to issue corporate equity in the form of shares as a means of raising capital
5. The ability to distribute earnings as dividends in relation to shares held
6. The facility for establishing management by the election of the Board of Directors with one vote by each voting share held, supplemented by the facility of proxy solicitation and proxy voting

Control of a corporation is secure only when more than 50% of the voting shares are held by an individual, another corporation or a controlling group. When shares of a corporation are publicly traded it is always possible for a minority group to attempt a take-over by obtaining more than 50% of the votes by either purchase or proxy. Good management should follow the trading in their company's shares very closely and investigate any peculiar increase in activity.

Basic corporation management structure

The ownership of a corporation and hence its management rests with the shareholders. Corporate law in most countries requires an annual shareholders' meeting at which time the shareholders elect the company Board of Directors to whom they then entrust the management of the company for the ensuing year.

The Board of Directors, while retaining the ultimate responsibility and authority, appoints a chairman of the board and the officers of the corporation. The officers vary with different corporations but usually consist of a president; vice-presidents of exploration, mining, production, and finance; treasurer; secretary; and controller. These officers are employees of the company while the members of the Board of Directors, as such, are not. It is possible, indeed usual, for certain directors to be officers and hence employees.

The Board of Directors may also appoint other committees which will have responsibilities for reporting directly back to it. Common use of this method includes the executive committee and the finance committee to which the board delegates certain specific authorities or which have legislated responsibilities. These committees will meet more frequently than the board and will provide each board member with a copy of the minutes of their meetings. A member of the Board of Directors should always insist on specific terms of reference and regular reports from such committees since the ultimate responsibility for their actions remains with the Board of Directors.

Another similar committee, now required by legislation in many countries, is the audit committee. This committee usually is composed of at least three directors the majority of whom are not officers or employees. One principal function of this committee is to provide a communication channel between the external auditor and the Board of Directors. The concept, purpose and duties of the audit committee are discussed in greater depth in Chapter 8.

An organization chart for most corporations would be similar to that shown in Fig. 1.1.

Corporate responsibilities

While a corporation has all the normal legal responsibilities to the general public, it has many other responsibilities which come under the stewardship of the Board of Directors and, from a more practical point of view, its officers.

While laws vary from country to country it is a virtually universal requirement that the shareholders be provided with an annual report of the company's affairs including a report from the Board of Directors and financial statements reported on by the external auditors. Many jurisdictions also require a semi-annual report from the directors together with an unaudited financial summary. In fact, a large number of corporations now report to their shareholders quarterly.

Securities commissions and stock exchanges also require periodic reports from corporations. In addition to specific statutory reporting requirements the principal criterion of such reporting can best be described as 'full, true, and timely disclosure'. The nature and timing of such reporting requirements are set out in the applicable security laws and stock exchange rules and regulations.

Directors' responsibilities

As a member of the Board of Directors an individual assumes an extremely serious responsibility. The responsibility and liability assumed is usually greater where the directorship is in a public company. The laws do not usually differentiate and the greater onus results only from a greater exposure than is experienced as a director of a private company. Directors owe their duty to the company rather

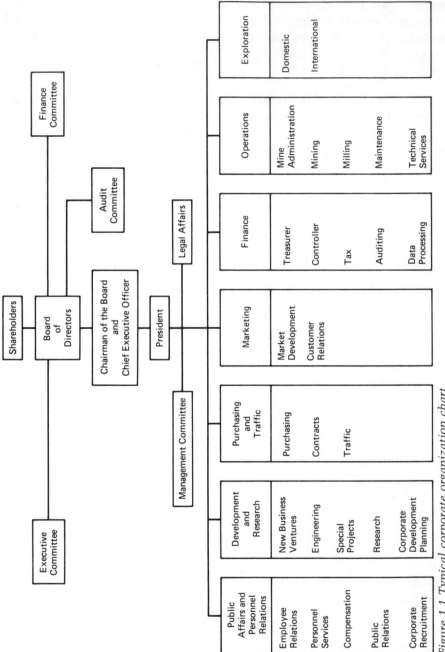

Figure 1.1 Typical corporate organization chart

than to any particular shareholder. Notwithstanding that a director may have been elected to represent a particular shareholder, his responsibility is to all shareholders. Directors may not consider the interests of anyone other than the shareholders except in such matters that may contribute to the general welfare of the company.

Over the past few decades corporate laws in many countries have been changed to introduce specific statutory duties and responsibilities of directors. Prior to the acceptance of a directorship each candidate is advised to seek counsel in order to be properly advised about the nature of the many responsibilities he will assume on acceptance of a directorship.

Corporate divisions

A division or department of a corporation is used as a means of isolating an operating, exploration or management function within the corporate entity. The concept of the single corporate entity does not change even if the divisional operation is separated in areas of physical location, management, accounting and nature of operations. The creation of a division is in fact a management tool designed to isolate and designate areas of responsibility without creating a new corporate entity. While the financial and other operations of the division are part of the corporation as a whole, effective management will assign objectives, budgets, reporting and management responsibilities to each division to measure the success or failure of that phase of operations in relation to specific objectives. A typical example of a divisional operation includes an exploration division and a specific mine operation division, each with its own management, responsibilities and objectives.

Segregation of operational and budgetary accounting controls by division is one of the primary means by which management can monitor the divisional operation.

Subsidiary corporations

A subsidiary corporation is a corporation in which the parent or holding company owns directly and/or indirectly through subsidiaries, shares carrying more than 50% of the votes which, if exercised, would elect a majority of the Board of Directors. While a subsidiary corporation is a separate legal and economic entity, its assets, liabilities, revenues and expenses must be consolidated with those of its parent companies for financial reporting purposes.

Generally a wholly owned subsidiary is used as an operating vehicle only when the following conditions are present and indicate certain advantages to the parent company:

1. Taxation
2. High-risk ventures where limitation of liability is desirable
3. Foreign operations
4. Regulated industries
5. Labour relations
6. Complete incompatibility of resources or accounting practices

A subsidiary whose shares are not wholly owned usually exists in that state for one or more of the following reasons:

1. The desired or agreed intent to have others hold a minority position in the equity
2. Equity fund raising from a minority group
3. Foreign policy relating to equity (e.g. Mexico)
4. Inability to acquire 100% equity when acquisition is made in the open market or in stages

As with a wholly owned subsidiary, a partially owned subsidiary (where more than 50% of the voting shares are held) should also be consolidated for financial reporting purposes. The only difference is the need to disclose separately the minority interest in shareholders' equity and to deduct the minority interest in determining net earnings.

Significant influence

One company may be able to exercise significant influence over the financial and operating decisions of another company even though it holds less than 50% of the voting shares. Significant influence is generally indicated by conditions such as representation on the board of directors, participation in policy making, material intercompany dealings, interchange of key personnel or provision of technical resources. From an accounting viewpoint, if a company holds less than 20% it is presumed that a significant influence does not exist unless such influence is clearly demonstrated. On the other hand, the holding of 20% or more does not in itself confirm the ability to exercise significant influence unless other positive indicators are present.

An investment which meets the significant influence criteria is almost always considered to be a long-term investment. The investor will, through its significant influence, have some degree of responsibility for its operations and management and therefore the return on its investment. It is appropriate that the proportionate share of income or loss be included in the results of the operations of the investor. This is equity accounting which is discussed further in Chapter 6.

JOINT VENTURES

Definition

A joint venture is a many-splendored thing and is said by some to defy definition. Others insist that it is a form of partnership. While the courts may ultimately determine the final nature of the beast, the following definition is one which best describes a joint venture from a practical point of view.

A joint venture is an association by agreement of two or more persons, partnerships or corporations entered into for the purpose of carrying out a specific business venture for profit, for which purpose they contribute their specified property, money, skill or knowledge. A joint venture is not a partnership; it is simply a contractual arrangement with the term 'Joint venture' being the most appropriate description.

While it is stipulated that a joint venture may not necessarily be an entity, the operations anticipated by the joint-venture agreement are often carried out by a corporation formed for that specific purpose. These corporate joint ventures will be governed by the joint-venture agreement which will usually dictate the voting control of the investors apart from the participation or equity in profits or losses.

Joint ventures may also carry on operations in a business style similar to a proprietorship or partnership. In this instance the parties to the joint venture may be sued for all liabilities of the joint venture with the right of recourse only to the other parties to the joint venture unless otherwise provided between themselves in the joint-venture agreement.

A joint-venture agreement should exhaustively dictate the provisions for:

1. The scope and duration of the venture
2. The ownership and ultimate disposition of assets
3. The determination of and equity in earnings and losses
4. Management and reporting policies
5. All other respective rights, contributions and obligations of the parties
6. Dissolution

Concept as an operating vehicle

With the tremendous increase in the cost of bringing a new mining property into production because of world-wide inflation, the general decrease in grades of ore, and the resultant increase in the tonnage requirements to make a project economical, many large new mining projects are operated on some kind of joint-venture basis. The facility of sharing risks, taxation, combining complementary technical knowledge and resources, and the avoidance of uneconomical duplicate facilities are only some of the operational advantages. The tremendous flexibility in the ownership and utilization of plant, equipment and mineral properties offers not only administrative advantages but also corporate tax advantages. The corporate joint venture also offers the advantage of limited liability to the participants.

With costs per ton of ore mined being so high, and with the tendency toward development in foreign countries, the trend is toward having one or more companies in the host country, as well as from other user countries, invest in the project. The financial reporting of these joint-venture operations is becoming increasingly important to mining companies.

From a management and operational viewpoint, the provisions of the joint-venture agreement are of particular significance. Joint ventures may be organized so that each investor may participate, directly or indirectly, in their management. While the overall management is dictated by the joint-venture agreement, the day-to-day management is usually delegated to one of the parties to the agreement. The relative risk of contributions to the venture will usually dictate the participants' interest in profits or losses.

Each joint-venture participant has the advantage of retaining those assets which it contributed on its own financial statements, provided title does not pass and provided appropriate disclosure is made of the use of those assets. The participants will, in many instances, take up their share of profits (or losses) on the equity basis (a single-line consolidation) with appropriate deductions for depreciation, amortization and depletion of contributed assets. In other circumstances it may be more appropriate to account for the investors' proportionate share of each of the assets, liabilities, revenues and expenses on a line-by-line basis called proportionate consolidation. Financial accounting for joint-venture interests is discussed in greater detail in Chapter 6.

OTHER ORGANIZATIONAL STRUCTURES

Proprietorships

A proprietorship is the simplest of organizational structures consisting of a single owner of an unincorporated business. A proprietorship may have a registered name (depending on the laws of the jurisdiction of operations), may have employees and may carry out any form of mining venture as is legally allowed by any other organizational structure.

While proprietorships do exist in certain isolated mining ventures, they are very rare. The difficulties and restrictions in raising funds, the horrors of unlimited liability and the disadvantages of high personal income tax rates discourage an individual from carrying on a mining venture in this manner.

Partnerships

As with proprietorships, the use of partnerships as a vehicle for the purpose of carrying on business in the mining industry is unusual. The reasons which discourage the use of this kind of organization are substantially the same as for proprietorships. Certain additional complexities are usually found in taxation of partners, depending of course on the tax laws of the country involved.

Occasionally one will find a corporate partnership engaged in mining activities. These partnerships are also rare and should not be confused with a corporate joint venture. In the case of a corporate partnership, the partnership will own the assets and incur the liabilities with each partner being jointly and severally liable for the partnership debts.

Some jurisdictions have partnership laws which allow the fairly extensive use of a special type of partnership known as a 'limited partnership'. This limited partnership usually has one or a very few general partners and a proportionately large number of limited partners. The general partners act as management and have the same responsibilities and liabilities as partners in an ordinary partnership. The limited partners are restricted in their liability to the amount of their capital and equity contribution. Again depending on the tax laws of the jurisdiction, certain tax advantages can be available to the limited deduction of partnership losses relating to exploration and property acquisition costs. The deductibility of these costs and the highly speculative nature of mineral exploration can make this organizational vehicle particularly attractive for mining ventures under the proper circumstances. Before using this type of vehicle individuals and corporations should be fully apprised of the tax laws applicable in the country in which they plan to operate.

A NEW PRIVATE MINING COMPANY

A discussion of business structures would not be complete without at least a general discussion of the process involved in the creation and financing of a new private (non-reporting) mining company. While the laws and procedures vary in different jurisdictions, the same overall concept is reasonably similar in most parts of the world. In any event, the principles discussed warrant the attention of management who should in turn seek the advice of legal counsel regarding the specific laws and procedures applicable in the jurisdiction of incorporation.

Incorporation

Initially, the owner of the mineral property must select a firm of solicitors. It is important to make this choice carefully. The solicitor should have some experience with mining companies,since mining securities law is relatively complex and the rules of application are becoming more comprehensive. The solicitor is primarily engaged to provide professional legal service to the company. Company solicitors are, however, very often valuable members of the Board of Directors because of their knowledge of corporate law and their familiarity with the agreements to which the company is a party.

There are numerous other factors on which professional advice should be sought before incorporation, as follows.

Jurisdiction of incorporation
Where a choice is possible, certain jurisdictions have advantages over others. Some countries allow incorporation under federal, state, provincial, district or territorial charters, the laws of which may differ with specific advantages and disadvantages to the objectives of the intended company.

Public or private company (reporting or non-reporting)
Under the provisions of some securities acts, a private company has a distinct advantage for a new mining company in that the private sale of shares does not require registration or a prospectus. In many instances this is appropriate since initial financing is obtained from personal friends and close business associates. The advantages and attributes of a private company usually disappear as soon as there are more than a

specified number of shareholders or there is an invitation to the public to subscribe for shares. A private company which is controlled by a public company will, in most jurisdictions, take on all the reporting requirements of its parent.

Directors
The directors of any company should be chosen with great care. Better no directors than silent or figurehead directors. A director should have some knowledge in the mining field but more important he should be comfortable with the purposes and prospects of the company and with his fellow board members. It is becoming increasingly important to include knowledgeable 'outside' people on the board. The audit committee requirement is just one reason. A director assumes a large responsibility and he should accept this fact or decline appointment.

Auditors
The choice of auditors is similar in many respects to the choice of the solicitor. The independence of the auditor is often dictated by law or his professional code of ethics, and that independence is vital to the performance of his duties. As with solicitors, an auditor who is familiar with the mining industry and the ways of securities commission and stock exchange can be of especial assistance both at the time of incorporation and in the future.

Other matters
The corporation will have to be given a name which is acceptable to the registration authorities. The objects and powers where required in the incorporation documents will have to be reviewed to insure compatibility with intended corporate objectives. A trust company should be selected to act as registrar and transfer agent for the capital stock. Printed share certificates in a form acceptable to both securities commissions and stock exchanges should be selected at the outset.

Capitalization

Capitalization is the term used to describe the nature, number and dollar amount of the shares of capital stock which a company is legally entitled to issue under corporate law. The authorized capital is the maximum number of shares, and sometimes value, which a company may issue. The issued capital is the shares actually issued and money received from such issue.

In establishing the authorized capital of a company two basic decisions must be made, the total number of shares to be authorized and the types of shares to be authorized.

The total number of authorized shares is of little consequence except in jurisdictions which assess a fee based on total authorized capital. A reasonable number of common shares from 2 million to 5 million is usual. Remember that the authorized capital can be changed at a later date. The minimum authorized should be at least sufficient to raise anticipated initial capital requirements.

The type of shares to be authorized presents a different problem in some areas. Authorized shares can be 'par value' shares or 'no par value' shares. Par value shares usually cannot be issued at a discount but can be issued at a premium. This presents a problem in instances where the par value and thus the initial issue is for instance $2 which, in a speculative venture, may prove more difficult to market than shares at a price of 50¢. On the other hand if par value shares are sold in excess of par there are no problems. The premium (price in excess of par) is part of shareholders' equity and is usually designated as contributed surplus or additional paid-in capital.

In the case of no par value shares, the issued capital of the company is usually deemed to be the amount for which the shares are issued as fully paid. This appears to be the most flexible route except in jurisdictions where a maximum issue price must be stated for no par value shares. Any issue in excess of the maximum authorized price will usually require an amendment to the corporate charter which will entail a shareholders' meeting, legal costs and quite probably additional registration fees.

As mentioned earlier, it is possible to structure the authorized capital to include shares with special conditions attached. The most common type of special condition share is the preferred share. Preferred shares are usually non-voting (except in some cases where dividends are in arrears) and do not participate in equity. Very often they are redeemable which makes them useful as a form of term debt. These shares usually have priority when dividends are distributed, are sometimes cumulative and occasionally are convertible to common shares based on a predetermined formula. Preferred shares are occasionally used by mining companies for intercorporate financing, especially in jurisdictions where intercorporate dividends are not taxable. In addition, redeemable preferred shares are not considered as a liability or debt which makes them attractive if maximum debt limits have been reached.

Some jurisdictions have adopted a standard fee for all incorporations regardless of capitalization while others have a policy of total aggregate consideration. These are some of the factors worth consideration in the choice of jurisdiction of incorporation.

Consideration on initial share issues

The mining property or rights must now be sold to the company, giving rise to the matter of appropriate consideration for them. It is important that the applicable securities law and/or policy statements be considered at this stage. While the securities commission may not yet be involved, the ultimate step of going public and the filing of a prospectus will place these transactions under its legal jurisdiction and scrutiny.

As previously discussed, the basic consideration received for a mining property does not necessarily represent value. It is impossible to value a property before considerable exploration has taken place. The key issue, in the case of a new company, there should be sufficient vendor shares issued to allow the property vendors to control the company, at least until an equal number of shares have been issued for cash. It is not uncommon to see the issue of 500 000 to 750 000 vendor shares issued for mineral properties as an initial corporate transaction. There are maximum limits set in certain jurisdictions.

Once the number of shares to be issued is determined an issue price must be assigned. Contrary to general belief it is possible to determine a price. There is always a dollar range within which a person would not dispose of a mineral property just as there is a dollar point when a sale would take place. This price determination is more difficult to make when dealing with a non-arms-length transaction. Therefore the basis for setting price is usually the number of shares involved with only secondary importance attached to the dollar amount ascribed. If a fair value cannot otherwise be determined, the fully paid issue price of the vendor shares should be the same price per share as the first shares issued for cash.

Shares are often issued in the early stage of corporate life as consideration for services, equipment or exploration work. Extreme caution must be exercised in the determination of the fair market value of goods and services before the issue price of shares is set. If shares have previously been issued for cash or if a cash issue is contemplated in the near future, then the actual or contemplated issue price will in most cases be acceptable. The directors should be careful to indicate the agreed purchase price of goods and/or services together with the 'fully paid' price of the shares issued in both the board minutes and the purchase agreement.

The vendor's pre-incorporation or pre-sale costs relating to the mineral properties are not usually paid back to the vendor unless an appropriate reduction is made in the number of vendor shares issued. The vendor shares are considered to be payment in full for the properties acquired. The exception to this rule is in the case of balances due to others under option and/or purchase agreements for additional claims included in the vendor agreement.

Private mine financing

Private mine financing is accomplished by what may loosely be termed a 'pre-public issue'. In jurisdictions where permitted this type of share issue may be made only by a private company. It eliminates the expense and delay of a prospectus, registration, etc. This relief from registration is allowed only in the case of a private company and will always be governed by the provisions of the pertinent company law. Private funds to an unlimited amount are often raised within this general framework, but they will always be limited to a small number of registered shareholders.

As a practical matter, regardless of law or jurisdiction, a private financing will be used only to raise relatively small amounts. It is hardly a substitute for the larger public financing which must be done within strict rules of securities laws.

Escrowed and pooled shares

While not applicable in all jurisdictions, the terms 'escrowed' and 'pooled' shares are common enough in the mining industry to warrant brief comment.

Escrowed shares usually denote the existence of an escrow agreement which will provide, in most cases, for the holding of a specified number of shares (usually all or most of the vendor shares issued for the original mineral properties) subject to periodic release only on fulfilment of prescribed conditions. Such conditions may include provisions for completion of specified exploration work, expenditure of specified sums on exploration, etc., as prescribed by a securities commission. It is possible that the escrowed shares may have to be gifted back to the company if the vendor property is abandoned. It is obvious that escrow conditions apply only to a public company, but the initial vendor shareholders in a private company should be very aware of escrow conditions which could be imposed at some future time.

The pooling of shares is an action outside the corporation between consenting shareholders. Pooling should be done only pursuant to a written agreement which should specify the number of shares to be pooled, the parties involved, voting conditions and the period of pooling. This device is usually used to ensure voting control and occasionally to prohibit the dumping or block sale of a significant number of shares which could destroy an otherwise orderly share market.

THE PUBLIC COMPANY

The issue of shares of capital stock of a mining company is probably the most common method of raising funds via the public purse. Public debt issues such as bonds and debentures are also a very common means of raising funds. The principal difference is that a share issue represents equity and other methods create a debt to be repaid with interest.

In order to tap the public purse a company must be a public company which, in general terms, means that it is registered as such with the appropriate governing bodies in its jurisdiction. Going and staying public commits a company to a multitude of complex laws, rules and reporting requirements. Expert advice is essential. While it is not possible or practical to describe in detail all the complexities involved, it is important that management of any mining company be familiar with at least the basic aspects of the rules within which the company will operate.

Governing bodies

While the form of the organizations which govern the legal and reporting requirements of a public company vary within English-speaking countries, their substance is the same. All such bodies require registration, reporting and compliance with the laws and rules which come under their administration. Essentially these organizations are the watchdogs for the public.

Probably the largest organization of this kind in the world is the Securities and Exchange Commission (SEC) in the United States. The SEC is an independent regulatory agency of the United States Government and exercises a quasi-judicial role in controlling the distribution and trading of securities (both equity and debt) within the United States.

In Canada the securities laws come within provincial jurisdiction. Each province has its own *Securities Act* and Securities Commission.

It is the commission which administers the Act and thus controls the distribution and trading of securities within its province. Extra-provincial registration is required for trading and distribution in more than one province. The securities laws are very similar in most provinces and the commissions have issued national policy statements to facilitate inter-provincial transactions.

In the United Kingdom a central body called the Stock Exchange serves as the administrator of the securities laws. The Stock Exchange is a self-governing body which also rules and regulates the stock brokerage firms who belong to it.

In Australia the registration, reporting and compliance with respect to securities issues and trading are governed by the *Companies Act*. The administration of the Act is carried out by the Corporate Affairs Commission. The Association of Australian Stock Exchanges is a self-governing body which comes under the jurisdiction of the *Companies Act*.

Registration and exchange listings

Every company that wishes to sell its shares or raise funds in public must be registered with the securities commission in the jurisdiction in which the issue is to take place. Once again the rules and procedures vary around the world, but the basic ground rules are similar. Probably the most stringent rules, including filing and reporting requirements, are prescribed by the SEC in the United States. In simple terms, registration takes place when the SEC accepts the Registration Statement of which a prospectus forms part. Regulation SX governs the form and content of documents and information to be filed as part of the registration process. Other jurisdictions in the world will have different forms and different rules but all will require similar long lists of data concerning corporate history, current operations, details of shares issued, debt structure, significant agreements and contracts, background information on directors plus the extent of their shareholdings, at least five years' comparative financial statements, etc.

The complexities of registration with the SEC and most other commissions or exchanges are such as to require the services of a corporation lawyer who is also a specialist in securities registration. It would be rare to achieve registration in the United States for less than $75 000–$100 000 as a minimum, with some registrations far exceeding that amount. The cost in other jurisdictions will vary with the degree of complexity.

A stock exchange is an organization which exists for the purpose of providing its members a common facility for buying, selling and trading in shares, bonds and, in some cases, commodities. The stock exchange is comprised of security dealers who usually have to purchase a 'seat' on the exchange in order to become a member and use the exchange facilities. The basic securities law of the jurisdiction and the securities commission will govern virtually all securities transactions, although a stock exchange may impose certain additional rules, registration, periodic filing requirements and a listing fee. In order to qualify its shares for public trading a mining company must first be registered with the securities commission and then be listed for trading on a stock exchange.

The prospectus

A prospectus is a complex document prepared by the company which must be filed with and approved by the securities commission before a company may issue shares or debt to the public. Essentially it is an offering document which will describe the securities offered for sale, the unit and total issue price, the company, its directors and officers, its operations, the use for which the funds are being raised and extensive technical and financial information. The form and content of a prospectus will be governed by the *Securities Act* or regulations of the jurisdiction of filing. It should be noted that a prospectus must contain full, plain and true disclosure with severe penalties imposed on any party failing to adhere to this principle.

It is rare that a prospectus is issued without the company first having entered into an agreement with a securities broker to market the securities or debt being offered. The securities broker will have a knowledge of the marketplace and be of invaluable assistance in determining an attractive and acceptable offering and the best price at which the issue can be sold. This price must be related to the total amount which management must raise to achieve its own objectives.

Other professional assistance will be required in the preparation of a prospectus. In addition to the obvious need for a law firm which can provide the highly specialized services required in preparing a prospectus, the company will almost certainly have to call on a firm of consulting engineers who will be required to give their independent opinion on the technical aspects of the project for which the funds are being raised. In addition, the company's external auditors must give their independent opinion on the financial statements and other related financial data contained in the prospectus. It should be noted that most securities commissions require a letter from the independent consulting engineers and auditors which will state that they have read the prospectus and consent to the use of their reports.

If a material change occurs in the company's rights, assets or obligations during the time that the prospectus is current, particularly while the sale of shares under the prospectus is in progress, it will be necessary to file an amendment. The filing of such an amendment is of the utmost urgency since failure to do so will result in a prospectus being in distribution which does not contain full, plain and true disclosure with the ultimate serious consequences for the directors or other parties to it.

In a situation where a specific project becomes impractical and is discontinued prior to completion, management may wish to utilize the funds remaining from a prospectus issue on an alternative project. In certain instances, it may be necessary to call a shareholders' meeting to obtain approval. This is required since the prospectus usually must state that the funds raised will not be used for a purpose other than indicated.

Underwritings

An underwriting, in most jurisdictions, will take the form of an agreement between a member of a recognized stock exchange and the company wishing to sell its shares to the public. The underwriter's business is selling securities and he will expect to be paid for this service.

The basic purpose of an underwriting is to raise funds for corporate purposes by the sale of shares or other securities. Underwritings will take various forms and be prepared to various degrees of sophistication depending on the company whose shares are being underwritten, the size and purpose of the underwriting and the requirements of the stock exchange and securities commission in the particular jurisdiction.

Payment to an underwriter can take several different forms including:

1. Commissions
2. Discounts
3. Share bonuses
4. Portion of escrow shares
5. Some combination of two or more of these

Underwritings may vary from a single lot, firm-price purchase to a firm-price with an option or options on further lots of shares by specified dates and at specified prices.

While many similar principles apply to most underwritings, large or small, greater caution and sophistication are necessary in a major issue of securities for projects requiring many million dollars. Feasibility and metallurgy reports will be checked and double-checked, market prices and sale contracts will be reviewed, independent mining consultants will be called for reports, and ore reserves will be investigated and re-calculated even to the point of further development work being insisted on. In essence, the underwriter must be satisfied with the underlying value of the product he is selling to his customer to protect his own reputation.

An underwriting is not necessarily restricted to the sale of shares. Bonds, debentures, income debentures, shares with warrants and any other permissible type of security may be sold through an underwriting. The funds to be raised will vary from smaller amounts ($150 000–$250 000) for speculative junior issues to many millions in senior issues. The company should exercise care in the selection of the underwriter who must be able to reach the proper type of market for the type of security being offered. It is not likely that a large, highly sophisticated senior brokerage firm would market a small junior issue nor would a smaller local firm normally have the resources to market a multimillion dollar issue. While there are notable exceptions, brokerage firms tend to specialize in the issues they underwrite and the market they reach.

CONCLUSION

The inner working of corporations and organizational structures can be either simple or complex, most often the latter. For this reason most mining companies of any size will have a corporate secretary and often at least one lawyer on staff, both of whom will be part of the management team and work very closely with the company's outside counsel.

Clearly decisions about business structures, capitalization, joint ventures, securities registration, prospectuses and underwritings should not be made by amateurs. I hope that the material in this chapter has provided mine management with some insight and understanding of this aspect of the business, for which management they are responsible.

2

PROPERTY SEARCH, ACQUISITION AND EXPLORATION

Few mines are found today by chipping away on a piece of surface outcrop. The individual prospector still finds some ore bodies, but because of ever-increasing costs the majority of present day prospecting and exploration is carried out by teams of highly skilled mine hunters using extremely sophisticated instruments. Each year an increasing majority of the new deposits are discovered by instruments which measure the earth's gravity, magnetism, electrical conductivity and radioactivity. Computers, through analysis of electronically stored geological data, are playing a growing role in exploration. Modern prospecting is a far cry from the days when rugged prospectors worked for months in the solitude of the wilderness with only elementary instruments and knowledge to guide them.

Despite all the technological advances, mineral search and exploration remains a very risky and expensive undertaking. It is not unusual for a mining company to spend $5–10 million or more on a property before it has sufficient information to determine whether the property is economically viable for mine development. Statistics indicate that for approximately every thousand exploration projects only one will become a mine.

The fundamental law of mineral economics dictates that the risks taken must be in balance with the potential profits. This chapter outlines some of the management tools and techniques used to minimize the financial risk in mineral search and exploration.

GRASS ROOTS EXPLORATION

For purposes of this discussion the term mineral search means the grass roots exploration process of identifying an area for evidence of mineralization worthy of acquisition and some degree of in-depth exploration. As with most businesses there will almost always be some overlap in operations in that search will involve an element of exploration and vice versa. This section deals with some of the finance-based considerations which will confront management with respect to property search and acquisition.

Corporate philosophy/policy

Every mining company, whether producing or exploring, has some form of corporate philosophy, a definition of what it wants to achieve and how it intends to achieve it. There are no rules for establishing a corporate policy but even a cursory examination of any successful business will produce evidence of some basic philosophy on which the corporate policy is based. As an exploration company, will you carry a project to the production stage, dispose of good exploration bets, or attempt a joint venture with some major? Will a company carry out all its own mineral search or examine properties brought to it by others or both? Is the company interested in large or small properties or both?

Wise and prudent management will attempt to codify and commit to writing their corporate policies and objectives, not to stand forever as rigid rules, but to set corporate goals and to achieve them in the most efficient manner possible.

Mineral property search

The search for mineral properties is not always distinguished from exploration in practice since both involve the quest for geological information which will ultimately lead to the acquisition of exploration rights in mineralized areas. Search will range from general observation and surveillance of industry activity to expensive detailed geological examination of specific geographical areas. The degree of effort and the methods employed vary widely from company to company, but some degree of continuing activity is essential to the survival of every mining company. Location of mineralized areas is a necessary preliminary to acquisition and exploration.

Mineral search in the initial stage will often involve the review of geological and topographical maps, and aerial photographs to reveal the presence of surface formations indicative of mineral deposits. The geologist will use geophysics and geochemistry to detect anomalous variations in gravity and magnetic forces of the subsurface and chemical content of soil and rock which may indicate the possibility of a mineral deposit. When the possibility of a mineral deposit is indicated, the rights to the mineralized area must be secured. <u>There may be some instances where ground is deliberately not acquired at the time of location in order to maintain secrecy and protect an exclusive within the area.</u> Property acquisition is discussed later in this chapter.

For budget and cost control purposes the following mineral search costs are usual and should be considered:

1. Salaries and related costs
2. Transportation
3. Equipment and supplies
4. Assay and analysis
5. Access to property (prior to acquisition)
6. Outside consultants
7. Geophysical–geochemical surveys
8. Report preparation

Search and acquisition criteria

It is important to decide on some basic property search and acquisition criteria for any given company. This can be determined only from the basic corporate policy and the response to a series of key questions:

1. What fixed or annual financial resources are available for property search and acquisition?
2. Does the company have adequate facilities and personnel to carry out its own search and acquisition program?
3. Should outside sources of mineral properties be utilized to maintain the company's inventory of properties available for exploration?
4. Is a search program necessary in light of all other circumstances? (e.g. existing inventory of unexplored properties, financial restrictions, availability of outside properties, etc.)
5. Is a majority interest in the property imperative?
6. Will foreign mineral properties be considered and, if so, in what priorities do foreign countries rank?
7. Does management have expert knowledge of matters in acceptable foreign countries relating to language, government stability, mining laws, taxes, foreign ownership, currency stability, repatriation of capital and income? If not, is management prepared to pay for expert advice?
8. Are particular types of mineral deposits of greater or lesser interest to the company? Why?

9. Are large, low-grade mineral deposits as acceptable a search target as small, high-grade deposits?
10. Are financial resources available to place a property in production or will the company retain an interest and allow a major to take over?
11. What is the minimum return on investment acceptable to management? Why?

There are undoubtedly many additional questions of a similar nature which will come to mind. Answers to these questions will provide management with a set of guidelines which will serve as a very valuable planning tool. Search and acquisition activities may then be directed towards specific and desirable goals and proper assessment may be made of both successes and failures. A series of other considerations relating to exploration criteria are discussed later in this chapter.

Geographic considerations

Under this broad heading come the basic questions relating to logistics, political stability, and taxation. Within any country, management must consider logistical questions such as availability of competent labour, transportation and shipping facilities, power and water supply. If logistical factors are not favourable it may be useless to search for a deposit which, if found, cannot be removed at a profit. In general, many logistical problems are solved if the deposit is near transportation.

A study of the political stability of the area being considered for mineral search must be made. Because of the large cost and extended period of time from discovery to production, reasonable stability is necessary. It is worthy of note, however, that often the exploration competition is far greater in an area which is politically stable. It may well be that companies with smaller exploration budgets will conclude that they have a greater chance of success in a country less stable politically but where the competition is less. The type of political stability should also be analysed. Is the instability temporary or permanent? (Instability in Chile may be temporary, but that in Cuba appears to be permanent.) It should also be remembered that many major mining companies have operated successfully and profitably for years in countries where political instability has existed for decades. Most mine managers would agree that the greater the degree of instability, the shorter the desired payback period. The degree of stability will have to be determined through analysis of conditions existing and anticipated at the time of the study of a particular country.

Taxation policy is probably one of the most complex and difficult problems facing any mining company looking at the possibility of mineral property acquisition in other countries. All forms of taxation (sales taxes, property taxes, inventory taxes, local income taxes, mining taxes, royalties and general income taxes) must be thoroughly studied. Methods and possible restrictions on repatriation of earnings and capital must also be investigated.

Property or corporate ownership control by foreigners is not permitted by some countries (such as Mexico). Other countries have special rules concerning dividends and taxation where foreign control is deemed to exist. Complete details of foreign policies of this nature are essential, and expert legal and financial advice should be sought.

Last, but not least, many smaller (and sometimes large) companies are not properly equipped to do business in a foreign country, particularly where different languages and customs exist. Initially this may not appear to be a major problem but often, when combined with different laws, business customs, other communication problems and great distance or time zone factors, the smaller organization should consider whether it is better off to confine its activities to its 'own back yard'.

PROPERTY RIGHTS AND RECORDS

Mineral rights

The right to explore, develop or mine a property can take many forms. The terminology used to describe these rights varies from country to country but basically the types of rights available are similar. Legal advice will almost always be necessary.

In unfamiliar jurisdictions management is well advised to take local legal advice relating to acquisition of short-term rights, governing legislation, tenure, work requirements, annual fees or taxes, recording time limit, claim number limit, prospecting and exploration licenses, mining licenses, transfer and/or sale restrictions, government interests such as ownership, royalties, etc., and availability of final or long-term title. It is also important to have a legal search for the possibility of special rights which may be held by others such as surface rights, precious metal rights, timber rights, etc.

The simplest form of a property interest is 100% ownership of the mineral claims, licenses or rights. In some jurisdictions outright ownership is rare or impossible. Most companies will either stake their own claims after prospecting or will purchase, or take an option to purchase, claims in an area of geological interest. Mineral claims usually represent a short-term interest. A long-term interest, such as a mineral lease, is not usually acquired until a major exploration program has been carried out and the related evaluation program indicates a strong possibility of an economic ore body. The conversion of short-term rights, such as a mineral claim, to a long-term lease will require a full property survey, usually at a substantial cost, which is not justified unless the property appears to be very promising or there is a legal dispute over the ground involved.

Claim control records

The maintenance of effective control and property records relating to mineral property rights is absolutely essential in any mining company. Sloppy property management has occasionally caused serious embarrassment to management and has cost many thousands of dollars to recover title to key claims which inadvertently have been allowed to lapse. Every mining company must have a proper claims control or properties record system with one individual responsible for providing timely advice to management regarding claims held, work or payment requirements, and expiry dates.

A claims control system can be simple (a manual card file) or complex (computerized) depending on the number of different properties. Regardless of the system used, the basic data to be recorded and periodically updated should include at least the property name, legal description, date of acquisition, nature of tenure (lease, ownership) and the next due date for work filing, lease payments or other similar requirements. The claims control clerk should provide the geological or other appropriate management department with written notices of claim expiry or other significant dates, giving several months or more lead time, in order that appropriate action can be taken. Details of work recorded, payments made, acquisitions and disposals should be provided to the claims control clerk on a regular, systematic basis.

The responsibility and authority to drop or abandon smaller properties or peripheral claims should rest with the senior exploration officer while the dropping of major properties should be approved by the Board of Directors. The disposition of properties should always be approved, in writing, by the responsible party. A copy of such approval should be retained as part of the claim control record system.

VALUATION OF MINERAL PROPERTIES

Mining rights are a unique class of asset. The ultimate value of an ore body can only be known in retrospect when it is exhausted. It is appropriate that some discussion be devoted to the practices used in the valuation of properties or rights for financial recording purposes, since they often represent the principal and sometimes the only major asset of an exploration or development company.

The determination of the physical quantity and grade of mineralized ore is not the only difficult problem. Constant changes in world supply, metal prices, and production costs result in a shifting of the borderline of what constitutes ore and waste. Technical changes, threat or outbreak of war, government action (taxation, incentives, etc.), ecological requirements and political stability add to the list of uncertainties any of which may have a long or short-term effect on the already extremely difficult problem of valuation of a mining right.

In spite of the foregoing, mineral properties and rights are purchased and sold and prices are established, most often on the basis of an arbitrary cash payment and/or a share interest plus a negotiated carried or working interest. Any outright property purchase or sale is usually based on some arbitrary basis of valuation negotiated between buyer and seller. Transactions of this nature are almost always restricted to properties that are in the very early stages of development where indications of mineralization are present but undefined.

Valuation of unexplored properties

Some arbitrary method may have to be used to record the value of unexplored mineral rights, provided that it is accepted that the amount recorded may not necessarily bear any relation to, or afford any indication of, the true present or ultimate value. The arbitrary methods, combinations or variations are summarized as follows:

1. Use a nominal value of $1 which is an acceptable convention when recording the existence of an asset of uncertain value.
2. Record the property at cost where cash or cash and shares represent the considerations.
3. When par value shares are used, multiply the number of shares issued to the vendor by their par value. This method is not acceptable unless no other method is available and is not much of an improvement on some figure simply picked at random.
4. In new companies where shares are issued for properties, use the

price at which the initial cash shares are issued. In existing companies use the price of shares issued for cash on or about the same date as the property acquisition or alternatively use the market price if the shares are traded.

The latter approach of applying a price to the shares, issued as full or partial consideration of mining rights, on the basis of the established current share trading value or price is the most acceptable practice for companies in the exploration stage. It follows the accepted criterion of using the best current information available at the time the asset is recorded. It must be emphasized that this is a method of recording a cost where a share valuation is involved and hence is a valuation process. As previously stated, unexplored mining rights are difficult to value in the normal sense and thus are very often purchased or sold with some form of carried or working interest. Carried and working interests are discussed later. It should also be remembered that in the initial stages of an exploration company the mineral property rights usually constitute the only significant asset which stands behind the shares for which the asset was acquired.

Other valuation matters

When mining rights are transferred between closely related companies, it is not uncommon for the value assigned (or cost attributed) by the purchaser to be the same as the recorded cost in the accounts of the vendor. Very often the determination of vendor cost will include exploration costs to date of sale in which case full and appropriate disclosure of the cost components will be required. Great care must be taken in using this method if a minority interest is present in either of the related companies since a price too high or too low will hurt or benefit the minority group. In an arms-length disposition where shares are the consideration, the current market value of shares issued or received is usually the only method of establishing price.

A degree of caution must be exercised if trading in the shares is highly speculative with inflated prices or is unusually depressed with low prices because of general market or economic conditions. Either of these conditions may reflect too specific a market price and result in a value being placed which is too high or too low. Under these circumstances a long-term average price per share may be more appropriate provided relatively stable conditions exist within the company during the averaging period.

In cases where a certain amount of exploration has been completed and a higher level of geological data is available it is possible to establish some form of market value for a mineral property. A geologist will usually be best qualified to perform this sort of valuation using estimated reserves, prices, costs and a reasonably high discount factor to relate to the high risk at this early stage of property development. Market value is the price for which a property may be sold in an arms-length transaction. Both buyer and seller will perform their own valuation exercises and the ultimate transaction price or true market value will be the price which they agree on. Market values must be established for joint ventures and other similar property development agreements. Where an outright purchase or sale takes place the 'market value' is usually the total price with payments staged on an option to continue basis, allowing the purchaser the right to abandon at his option without further risk or obligation.

The cost of mining rights (and the related exploration and administrative costs) should be written off if the properties are abandoned or if the decision to abandon is made, whichever is the earlier. In non-operating companies the write-off is a loss resulting in a deficit or reduction in retained earnings, if any, while in operating companies the charge is against current earnings. In many countries search and exploration costs are expensed as incurred. The timing of write-offs will depend on the accounting policies within the jurisdiction and the company's own stated accounting policy.

EXPLORATION

In order to understand the management and financial control concepts relating to mineral exploration discussed here, it is first necessary to define the word exploration as it is used in the following pages. There are various stages of exploration from grass roots programs designed to locate an area of geological interest in remote areas to very definitive drilling and related programs designed to determine whether an economic ore body exists. Exploration such as ground prospecting and geophysics will often be done prior to property acquisition, particularly if the area is remote. The term exploration as used here describes the third stage of mineral exploitation which occurs immediately after (1) property search and (2) acquisition but prior to (4) development.

Exploration may also be described as the process by which management determines whether the mineralized area or anomaly constitutes an economic ore body. Naturally there is some overlap of search into exploration and exploration into development. It is not possible to define any phase of exploration sufficiently precisely to eliminate this overlap. Management should be aware of the necessity to devote proper time and attention to the distinction between these stages of mineral exploitation. To emphasize this point consider the probable waste of time, energy and funds if development begins prior to proper evaluation of exploration or if exploration begins prior to property acquisition. Significant second-stage objectives should not be pursued prior to proper levels of completion and evaluation of the first stage. It is imperative that management establish exploitation objectives and criteria and that it adhere to these. Deviations should be made only with complete awareness of the alternatives and possible consequences.

Exploration is the most basic and financially risky stage of the mining business. Exploration costs have risen drastically in the past decade with the cost of unsuccessful initial exploration programs often in the $100 000 plus range. Extensive programs can run into several millions of dollars. A great deal of management time must be spent considering the many factors which must be analyzed when deciding whether to initiate an exploration program and whether (and when) to terminate the program. The financial consequences can be significant.

Exploration criteria

A mineral deposit of sufficient size and grade can always be exploited; however, the chances of finding a large high-grade deposit are substantially less than those of finding a large low-grade deposit. There are many easily found deposits which because of size and/or grade cannot be mined at a profit. It is essential that management establish some criteria based on corporate philosophy which must be met prior to the start of any exploration program. Assuming that the grass roots exploration findings indicate a mineralized area worthy of further exploration there are other financial considerations which should logically come under review at this time. Aside from the geological considerations, other matters which should be considered in conjunction with the corporate policy base include the exploration budget, target minerals, and whether to hold, sell or joint venture the project.

Exploration budget
Corporate exploration budgets will vary from very large to very small amounts depending, once again, on management philosophy and the financial resources available. Exploration must continue, for without it there would be no new mines. The question which frequently arises

is whether the budget is designed to fit the contemplated exploration program or the program is designed to fit the budget. Do you budget on the basis that nothing will be found or do you assume that something will be found? Most often the budget is based on a combination of both factors. In the event of an apparent major discovery, management must be prepared to reallocate budgeted funds from other projects. Major finds cannot be planned and a high degree of flexibility is essential.

Since management is responsible to the Board of Directors and the shareholders for the progress of the organization, it is management's job to ensure that a proper and reasonable allocation of funds is made for exploration activities. The criteria for this will change from time to time depending on the profitability of other operations, access to equity capital, existing development commitments, general economic conditions and the desired or historical corporate dividend policy. It is important too that management plan for future exploration and that financial resources be reserved to carry out these programs. If existing resources are small it may well be that smaller targets will be set. On the other hand, some form of joint venture relationship may better serve the corporate purpose. On very large projects it is not uncommon for two or more majors to enter some form of joint venture.

As with all budgets there must be responsibility accounting. The exploration must establish and adhere to an exploration budget which has executive approval. Most exploration programs are staged or phased with evaluation taking place between stages. Budgets should also be staged for ease of monitoring. Budgets not only establish the financial parameters of an exploration program but also guide management in ensuring that financial resources are available as required.

Target minerals

The question of which type of mineral to search for is extremely difficult to answer. Each organization will reach its own conclusions for its own reasons and only the passage of a long time period will allow assessment of their individual judgement and degree of success. Should a company confine its operations to one or two basic metals, or does this matter? There is often a lag of several years between exploration and production. It is therefore somewhat hazardous to confine exploration to metals in short supply and at high prices. Management occasionally will engage outside experts to study the commodity markets in an effort to determine the type of mineral for which to explore. The advice of such experts should be used as a guide only. If they provided infallible information, a greater return (with less risk) could be obtained by playing the commodity futures market. Predictions of this nature are purely speculative. Management might place greater emphasis on the probable trend of metal prices in relation to major producer or world production costs. Prices will undoubtedly fluctuate on both sides of this scale, sometimes very widely. A vivid example is the price range of copper in 1973–74, rising from 50¢ to over $1.40 in a period of less than a year, then dropping by 60¢ in a period of about three months. Consideration must also be given to the cyclical nature of many metal prices as well as to the assessment of the profitability of deposits at various possible future price levels. There are obviously no hard, fast rules or guidelines for commodity selection. In summary, management should at least consider and evaluate the known world reserves of a particular mineral, producer cost and metal price trends, demand trends, new markets, inventory stockpile fluctuations, similar mines being readied for production and, lastly, the degree of their own internal expertise to explore, mine and market the mineral product involved.

Hold, sell or joint venture

There are many routes management may take with new property finds or established areas. Simply to hold the property is the obvious first consideration. Properties are most often held for future exploration when the financial resources currently available do not allow an exploration program to begin immediately. Some programs are suspended for reallocation of resources to a very high priority project. Other programs are suspended or postponed pending settlement of economic events. This happened with uranium properties in the late 1950s and with some coal properties in the 1970s. Properties adjacent to those under heavy exploration by others are often held pending their findings. While the primary decision to hold must have a sound geological base, management should not ignore the financial aspect, especially holding costs. While dollars spent are usually considered sunk costs it should be remembered that money has a time value. If a property can be sold there are often some good reasons to do just that.

The first concern of any company contemplating a property sale is whether they can recover their costs to date and whether the price may be a 'give away'. Management must consider the potential impact of spending further exploration dollars. Good results may bring a higher price or result in a hold. Bad results may result in a lower price or abandonment. Why consider a sale in any event? There are many reasons. The property may be too large, too small, or outside the minerals targeted. Funds may be required for diversion to other projects with higher priorities. Unless the property fits within the exploration criteria, management should always be alert to the possibility of a sale.

While there are some good reasons to sell a property outright, there are often better reasons to enter into some form of exploration agreement with another interested company. A common method of doing this is via a joint-venture agreement. A joint venture or other similar arrangement will allow retention of at least some interest in the property, while the other company earns its interest in the property by spending exploration dollars on the project. Joint ventures not only allow the spreading of risk but also allow participation in larger, more costly ventures than might otherwise be possible. Contiguous properties owned by separate companies are often best exploited by means of a joint venture.

It is sufficient to say that without some corporate policy or criteria, without the company knowing where it wants to go or how it intends to get there, the chances of corporate success are greatly diminished. The establishment of criteria such as exploration budgets, target minerals, and whether to hold, sell or joint venture the property are simple management tools which will not guarantee but will greatly enhance the possibility of positive financial achievement.

Preliminary exploration

During the past decade there has been a general but noticeable change in exploration emphasis with respect to the type of mineral deposit being explored. With some notable exceptions, many of the new mines involve large tonnage operations having a relatively small profit per ton. This type of operation can yield substantial long-term earnings, often far greater than a small tonnage, high-grade operation. Because of the longer mine life and greater number of variables such as metal price, operating costs, ore grades, and even reserves, the risk can also be higher unless substantially greater care is taken in the overall project evaluation. Small unit losses on a large tonnage operation can result in financial disaster, particularly when one considers that the present capital outlay for this type of operation may range from $75 million to $300 million and more. In this context, the importance of the initial examination of a new property cannot be overemphasized.

There are some very basic guidelines which management should follow in maintaining financial control in the conduct of an exploration program. Aside from technical approach as to methods of exploration, it is recommended that management:

1. Budget the number of properties to be examined.
2. Assess the potential property in light of the exploration criteria of the company.
3. Commit itself to the necessary short or long-term expenditures which may be required to adequately examine and assess the property.
4. Place the responsibility for the exploration project in the hands of a competent geologist giving him sufficient authority and access to management guidelines to carry out his responsibility.
5. In conjunction with the geologist, plan the exploration program in phases, including budgets, with each successive phase depending on the success or findings of the last. The geologist should be responsible for reporting recommendations to management and maintaining costs within budget limits.
6. Be prepared to drop the program, dispose of the property, or joint venture if the geologist so recommends.

Any geologist will thrive on the opportunity to conduct the exploration of a good property, but enthusiasm is inevitably replaced with indifference if he is saddled with the lengthy exploration of a poor property. It should be management's aim to create a deep personal interest on the part of the geologist. It is this approach which will allow management to best achieve its own objectives. Very often exploration personnel are provided with incentives such as bonuses or stock options as a means of stimulation.

Exploration for feasibility

As soon as any reasonably accurate data on the size, type and grade of an ore deposit are available, a preliminary feasibility study should be initiated to estimate operating costs, capital requirements, profit projections and cash flow. Even though such a preliminary study will be based on incomplete data, it may reveal a fatal economic weakness in the proposed plan. If such findings do not precipitate termination of exploration before the expenditure of larger sums, they will at least make management aware of the increased risk of an unsuccessful venture. If the initial findings of the preliminary study are promising, and as additional and more reliable data become available, new capital and operating costs must be calculated with constant appraisal being made of the potential for success. Many changes and adjustments will be made in the course of preparation of the final feasibility study. These are discussed at length in Chapter 4.

It should be noted that all exploration on any given deposit is for the purpose of determining the feasibility of the project. The entire object of exploring a mineralized area is to provide management with the most complete and accurate geological data possible, for it is this material which forms the cornerstone on which the ultimate decision to place the property in production is founded.

It is not the purpose of exploration to find a mineral deposit without exploiting it, therefore it is imperative that before extensive exploration or development expenditures are made management calculate the probable pay-out period under various conditions. Fluctuating metal prices represent the most significant unknown long-term factor in the preparation of any feasibility study. The net present value of future earnings decreases as interest rates increase. It follows therefore that high interest rates will play a major role in determining the time which can elapse between a major exploration program and production. A long delay may seriously impair future profitability. Both management and the geologist should consider the net present value of future earnings as a major factor in assessing the value of ore reserves and in exploration programming. Present values are discussed further in Chapter 3.

Exploration accounting and controls

There is an extensive variety of policies in accounting for mineral exploration costs, not only between non-producing and producing companies but also among producing companies.

In the United States exploration costs are usually expensed as they are incurred. In other jurisdictions some non-producing companies follow the policy of deferring all exploration costs until such time as the properties are brought to production or abandoned. If production is achieved these deferred costs are amortized on some appropriate basis as a charge against earnings. If the properties are abandoned, the costs, including any related deferred administrative costs, are written off. (In the United States all costs must be written off against earnings since charges to retained earnings are prohibited.) There is little logic in the deferral of exploration costs if one bears in mind the distinction between exploration and development. The underlying principle of deferral is that the costs deferred will ultimately result in future revenue and will be charged against that revenue as part of the conventional accounting process of matching costs and revenues. How this concept of deferring exploration costs came to be accepted in the beginning or why it is accepted now is difficult to understand since it is based on nothing but the simple expectation of success. Statistics indicate very clearly that the odds of an exploration project becoming a producing mine are extremely low. So far, however, the policy is acceptable and even some non-producing mines follow it in the United States.

A majority of producing mines follow the policy of expensing all exploration costs in the year in which they are incurred, as is the general policy for most mines in the United States. Some companies following this policy then reinstate and capitalize these costs at a later date if the project is brought to production. The amount reinstated is taken back into income in the year the production determination is made. The object or benefits of this exercise are somewhat obscure. A much smaller group of major producers in some jurisdictions defer all costs, and when property evaluation is complete, capitalize successful projects and charge unsuccessful projects to income. The disclosure of corporate accounting policies by major producers at least provides some opportunity for comparison. Most jurisdictions require, by law, the disclosure of accounting policies.

Exploration costs include items such as assaying, communications, consulting, drifting, drilling, engineering fees and expenses, field expenses, geological, geochemical and geophysical costs and expenses, government fees and taxes, licenses and permits, line cutting, pilot plants, salaries, shaft sinking, surveying (airborne, magnetometer, etc.) transportation, vehicle operation and other appropriate cost headings. All companies should prepare budgets and costs by particular property group in order to identify, both currently and in the future, specific project costs. Properties are often disposed of for shares in other companies and the exploration costs incurred may form the basis for establishing the cost of shares acquired. Where the deferral policy is followed by non-producing companies it is highly desirable that at least total costs by property group be disclosed to shareholders.

In the full-cost method all exploration costs, whether successful or not, are capitalized for amortization against the revenues obtained from the total corporate exploration effort on the basis that this results in a proper matching. This concept is followed to some extent in the petroleum industry but is not generally accepted in the mining industry. A large number of petroleum companies use the successful efforts method. The cost centre in mineral exploration is usually limited to a specific relatively small area and more often to a group of contiguous claims. Where the deferral policy exists, costs are written off only when the entire property is abandoned. The abandonment of isolated claims within the group should not precipitate a write-off unless it coincides with a decision to abandon the entire property.

This raises the question of what constitutes abandonment. It is obvious that if the legal interest is terminated, there is abandonment. There has been some reluctance to recognize abandonment where work is stopped. The company has decided to abandon, but the property rights continue for several years. This latter practice is now followed only where work is terminated without a decision to abandon. Disclosure of work stoppage and the property status should be mandatory where amounts involved are material.

The accumulation of exploration costs in the books of account is a mechanical process and serves only to provide management with an historical record of costs to a specified date. It is important that these costs are properly recorded and that proper monthly field reporting exists, including amounts paid, payable and committed. It is more important, however, that management be aware of what exploration costs are anticipated. This can only be accomplished through the preparation and proper use of exploration budgets.

If a budget is to work, responsibility must be assigned. The exploration project should be divided into phases or stages and the budget should be prepared on this staged basis by the exploration manager and senior field geologist who will have the ultimate responsibility for adherence. Management can hardly expect responsibility in the proper sense if the guidelines laid down are not acceptable to the geologist from the outset. Management then has the responsibility of providing the geologist with a record of his progress, whether a success or failure. The geologist should be requested to explain material deviations from budget. If exploration cost controls are to be effective, effort will be required on the part of both management and field staff. In order to extract this effort, the budget and related reporting must be considered important and be used. Otherwise the total effort is lost leaving just another pile of waste paper.

Good management will use proper exploration accounting as a tool to assess past performance and improve future performance. Their stewardship over corporate funds allocated for exploration extends not only to the control of total expenditures but also to the results obtained. The proper and logical selection of properties, the careful determination of search and exploration criteria, and the planning and control of expenditures will assist greatly in achieving desired management objectives.

CONTRACTUAL ARRANGEMENTS

The nature of the mining industry is such that sooner or later every company enters an agreement with a property owner, an exploration company or a producing mine for the acquisition or sale of mining rights. The purpose of this section is to review the more usual types of contractual arrangements and point out the aspects of critical interest and importance to both parties. It is essential and fundamental that every agreement relating to a mining right be treated as though a producing mine will result. An attempt should be made to cover every possible contingency with absolutely nothing left to chance. A thorough knowledge of the laws of partnership, securities, tax and property within the applicable jurisdiction is imperative. If agreements are drawn by in-house counsel then they should be reviewed by outside counsel and vice versa. A second opinion may save untold troubles in the future. Accounting and tax reviews of draft agreements are also imperative. Many individuals and companies have lived to regret their failure to adhere to the principle that 'an ounce of prevention is worth a pound of cure', since in many instances the error is terminal. Once a basic form of agreement is drawn it will undoubtedly serve in other similar circumstances, but caution should prevail.

The purchase or sale of a mining property or right may take the form of an outright deal or of an option. In the case of an outright purchase or sale the transaction is usually straightforward with nothing more required than execution and filing the appropriate form of bill of sale or transfer. In some circumstances the vendor will require a commitment of work by the purchaser and a return of title if the purchaser decides to abandon the project. These situations will require a contract or agreement of sale. The most popular and widely used method of acquiring or disposing of mineral rights is by way of option. The primary distinction between an outright sale and a sale by option is that in a sale title and beneficial interest pass at the date of the transaction, while under a sale by option title and interest pass at some future date with the sale subject to compliance with the option terms and conditions. Option agreements are discussed in some detail later.

Prospecting agreements

Mine finding has grown sophisticated and expensive. Most mining companies have their own mineral search or exploration departments.

There are, however, still many individuals searching for minerals so, while not too common, it is appropriate to discuss briefly the sorts of agreement used in these situations.

In many instances it is to the advantage of smaller mining companies and independent prospectors to pool their resources and broaden their opportunities by entering into some form of prospecting agreement. A wide variety of contractual arrangements have been used over the years involving partnerships, syndicates, employee relationships and grubstakes:

1. Partnership arrangements are not widely used or recommended since they involve all partners in the partnership liabilities. Limited partnerships are used in some jurisdictions where personal tax advantages accrue. In most instances partnerships of any nature are less flexible than a limited liability company and are often as expensive to organize.

2. Syndicate agreements were very popular at one time. The syndicate capital was divided into units which determined the proportionate equity of the unit holders. Most syndicates were formed for a specific purpose and for a specific time and the prospector undertook to explore a given area and acquire mining rights if mineralization was found. Securities law limiting and restricting the number of unit holders and the manner of unit sales has resulted in the decreased popularity of syndicates.

3. Grubstake agreements were used fairly extensively at one time for prospector financing. The high cost of searching remote areas now greatly restricts the individual prospector. As with most good arrangements, simplicity would prevail in a grubstake agreement. The usual terms provided for the prospector to prospect in a particular area and acquire property rights. In return for the advance of expense funds the grubstakers were entitled to a percentage interest in claims acquired. Grubstake agreements were for a limited time, usually one prospecting season.

4. Employee relationships are very straightforward in that the prospector simply becomes an employee of the mining company with the agreement being the terms of employment. Care should be taken by both parties to ensure that a grubstake agreement does not constitute an employment contract. Where employment exists the employer/grubstaker is responsible for such costs as unemployment insurance, workmen's compensation and public liability. Whether the prospector is an independent contractor or an employee is a

question of mixed fact and law, and caution should be exercised to ensure the desired arrangement exists.

Whatever the title or specific terms, the prospecting agreement should cover at least the following points:

1. Term of agreement
2. Authority to deal with the properties
3. Interests of the parties
4. Area to be prospected
5. Prospector's remuneration
6. Termination provisions

Vendor interests

It is not uncommon for a vendor of mineral rights to retain some form of interest in the rights sold. These retained rights are often in addition to an initial payment of cash and/or shares. The most common forms of retained interests are:

1. An undivided interest which is physical ownership of an undefined part of a specific claim or claim group. Without an agreement to the contrary a claim cannot be sold unless 100% of the parties holding such an interest consent to the sale.
2. A participating or working interest indicates that at some time the vendor must contribute to exploration and development costs in order to maintain his interest. This usually means that the purchaser will fund the initial exploration program. After a stipulated time or expenditure, the vendor must then contribute his share of costs or have his interest diluted in some relation to the amounts which he fails to contribute. It is evident that in a major find the working interest could be quickly eroded; to prevent this it is usual to include a minimum dilution limit in this type of agreement.
3. A non-assessable or carried interest is one where the holder has a free ride through the exploration and development of the mineral rights. Such an interest is usually smaller than it might be if it was a working interest. In some instances the carried interest is tiered. The vendor would have small carried interest until the other party recovers all its expenditures from the sale of the property or from production. At such time as full recovery is made the carried interest would then increase to some stipulated higher amount.

Vendor interests sometimes are a combination of the foregoing. An undivided non-assessable interest is probably the most common example. In any event it is imperative that great care be taken to understand properly and define the vendor interest in the agreement.

Purchase options

The principal feature of an option to purchase a mineral right is that the optionee obtains the exclusive right to explore and develop the property as long as the option agreement is in force. The optionee thereby has the opportunity to assess the economic potential of the property before he decides whether to drop the option or make the next payment.

The amount and nature of the total purchase price and the amount and timing of the option payments will be a matter of negotiation. Option agreements often include some form of minimum exploration covenants at least to keep the property in good standing. The option payment structure should be designed to allow sufficient time between payments for adequate exploration and assessment to permit justification of the next option payment. Payments are usually on a sliding scale with lower payments in the earlier stages and higher payments in the later stages.

The normal purchase option contains specific provisions such as:

1. Title representations and warranties stipulating valid location and recording and that the properties are in good standing for a specified period of time with no other person or company having any interest or right to the property.
2. Option payments specifying individual and total amounts together with due dates. A payment on signing is usual.
3. Termination provisions and in particular an automatic provision so that no notice is required by either party.
4. Access and data covenants which give the optionor reasonable access to the property and technical data during the option period and provide that copies of such data will be provided to the optionor if the option is terminated.
5. Property covenants assuring the optionor that the property will be kept in good standing, free of liens and encumbrances and, if the option is terminated, that all properties including additional properties or rights wthin a specified peripheral area will be returned in good standing for a stipulated period after termination.
6. Removal of building machinery and equipment after termination

within a stipulated time period should be provided for, failure to adhere resulting in passage of title to the optionor.

7. A covenant to comply with local laws and ecological requirements.
8. Claims relocation rights, including abandonment provisions, should be granted on written request or specified notice given by the optionee.
9. Property transfers should be executed and deposited with an escrow agent who will
   (a) deliver same to the optionee within a stipulated period of time after receipt of notice from the optionee that the final payment has been made or
   (b) return title to the optionor upon termination or default.
10. Escrow agents should be neutral parties, usually a trust company, and should be given specific written instructions agreed to and signed by both the optionor and optionee, usually as part of the purchase option agreement.
11. Minimum work commitments are often required by the optionor to discourage the optionee from simply sitting on the property and doing little or no exploration.

Working options

Virtually all provisions of the purchase option also apply to the working option. In fact one is a variation of the other and together they may take innumerable forms. The working option is most often used when a property is optioned to a larger, established mining company, usually called a 'major'.

A typical working option will, in addition to most of the provisions of a purchase option, provide for specified exploration work and/or specified expenditures on the property. At some point in time, usually after a stipulated minimum expenditure, the major will have the right to incorporate a company to which the property will be transferred. The interest in the new company will be divided between the optionor and the major in the agreed ratio. These ratios vary from deal to deal, but a 75:25 major to vendor ratio is not uncommon. Under this arrangement the major will advance all exploration capital and will be reimbursed out of the first production proceeds (or, as subrogated to other preferred debt) or proceeds from disposition of the property. It is important to the vendor to know and have stipulated the nature and jurisdiction of the new company to be incorporated. The vendor will naturally prefer a publicly listed company since this will allow greater liquidity and flexibility in dealing with his interest. It is not unusual for the major to insist on the right of first refusal on the vendor's interest.

Terms of working options vary, and often, instead of a new company being formed, the major will acquire the property and pay the vendor its interest as a percentage of net profits out of production, a royalty, or some other defined method of payment. In some cases the major will insist on the right to buy out the vendor completely at some predetermined price or agreed formula. Whether it is used or not, this type of provision should be included in every working option. In other instances where the vendor's interest is large, say 40%, it is not unusual for the agreement to provide that the vendor contribute by way of loan or capital to the cost of development and the physical plant. Whether the vendor contributes to cost or not, he will certainly be required to pledge his interest in the property as security for any third party debt required to place the property in production.

A working option agreement should contain virtually all the provisions of a purchase option agreement plus specific and detailed provisions for the following:

1. Minimum exploration expenditures and/or work commitments by the major setting out details, amounts and dates.
2. Provision for cash payments to the vendor in lieu of exploration or work to prevent default.
3. Definition of terms such as expenditure, exploration, development, preproduction period and other applicable terminology.
4. Provision for arbitration in the event of misunderstanding or disagreement between the parties including the appointment of an arbitrator or arbitrators.
5. Definition of the vendor's interest, and if it is based on or relates to a percentage of net profits from production, then the agreement should include a detailed and specific definition as to the calculation. A clear understanding is required of key items such as income taxes, interest, interest rates, management fees and non-cash charges such as depreciation of plant and equipment and amortization of exploration and development prior to production. Determination of these amounts and the underlying principles are basically accounting matters and it is strongly recommended that independent accounting advice be received prior to the signing of the final agreement.
6. Repayment of loans or advances from both the major and the vendor

should be clearly defined including the source of repayment funds, interest rates, the calculation of the loans and priorities for repayment.

7. Incorporation particulars, including place, jurisdiction and time of incorporation. Details of capitalization, public or private company, directorships, dilution and anti-dilution clauses, voting or non-voting shares and dividend policy and restrictions should all be clearly detailed in situations where a new corporation is to be used or is contemplated.

8. Default and termination provisions, including final ownership or disposition of assets, are imperative in any working option agreement.

9. Sundry provisions dealing with such matters as losses in net profit-sharing agreements, provision for pledging of interest as security for financing, and buy-out or rights of first refusal provisions should all be considered.

All the foregoing may appear over-complex and detailed for a 'simple property deal', but, if one will learn from the folly of others, these matters must be dealt with properly before the property is determined to be a producer.

SUMMARY

The mining industry is one of the higher risk businesses in existence today. The current high cost of search, acquisition and exploration is enough to stagger the imagination of even those experienced within the industry. While it is clearly acknowledged that the expertise of mine-making lies with the geologists and engineers, it should not be forgotten that risk is always ultimately measured in dollars. A management team that is aware and informed of the financial considerations, tools and techniques related to this aspect of the industry will better serve its company's objectives.

3

PROJECT SELECTION AND RISK EVALUATION

Virtually all business decisions are made with a financial motive in mind, and all business planning ultimately involves financial planning. From the inception of a business and throughout its life the decisions that determine its course are based on forecasts of economic events. This forecasting is performed in many ways, ranging from hunches and rules of thumb to simple or complex logical economic forecasts. It is the manner in which these forecasts are made and the management tools used in this process which will inevitably distinguish good management from bad. Only with a full knowledge and understanding of all risk factors can management properly evaluate a proposal and its alternatives and thereby make proper business decisions.

The purpose of this chapter is to review various methods used by mine management in selecting development projects and analyzing risk. It is important to note that no single forecast, analysis, study will necessarily provide all the answers which may be required to make a decision. Management should also bear in mind that for each decision there is always an alternative which in most cases is to do nothing, a decision which is often the most difficult to make.

PROJECT SELECTION CRITERIA

Management decisions in project selection involve the process of choosing between two or more alternatives based on some tangible measurement of economic return mixed with some intangible elements which cannot be quantified. The expenditure of funds on any mining project is undertaken to produce the desired economic benefit, earning a profit on funds invested. The ranking of projects strictly by evaluation of incremental monetary benefits is difficult. There is a large element of risk in the forecasting of the variables involved in any mining project. Even the determination of the desired rate of return on an investment is subject to examination depending on management's views on the market value of their stock, profit level and trends, and dividend policies. The mining executive investigating the potential return on a project must recognize the uncertainties even to the point of quantification within maximum and minimum limits as discussed later in this chapter. Within these limits there are various tangible methods available to management for comparing projects against each other and against corporate or industry investment standards. These methods use facts and assumptions to allow judgements on the desirability of project selections based on explicit measurement of economic events. The data provided by this measurement process form part of such project selection criteria as the relationship among cash flow, income and investments. It must be emphasized that the various methods of measuring economic returns provide data only and do not provide infallible criteria for project selection. Careful comparison, review of methods and applicability, together with evaluation of alternatives and confidence factors, are an integral part of the selection process.

Project ranking

Project cash flows and periodic net incomes are the principal input factors used in determining criteria for evaluation of a project. In order to derive these factors the project investment, production, revenue, and operating costs must be estimated and depreciation, amortization and income taxes calculated to produce the estimated financial results for the project. A simplified example distinguishing net earnings from cash flow is shown in Table 3.1.

The statement of net earnings and cash flow is part of the normal product of a feasibility study and is subject to all the variables and error factors inherent in it. Feasibility studies are discussed in Chapter 4.

Some of the methods of evaluating projects are as follows.

Hoskold method
This is an older method which assumes that a firm establishes a sinking fund to yield the initial investment by project termination and also desires a speculative return. The speculative return is calculated at a risk rate of return to reflect the nature of the project and the

TABLE 3.1

Net earnings and cash flow

		$
Net concentrate		80 000
Production costs		60 000
		20 000
Administration	2 400	
Interest	1 500	
Depreciation	3 500	
Amortization	1 000	8 400
		11 600
Taxes on income		
Current	1 000	
Deferred	4 800	5 800
Net earnings		5 800
Add back non-cash charges:		
Depreciation	3 500	
Amortization	1 000	
Taxes – deferred	4 800	9 300
Cash flow (available for debt, capital expansion, dividends, etc.)		15 100

sinking fund is deemed invested at a safe rate of return. The speculative return is calculated on the initial investment and is not reduced as this investment is recovered. The Hoskold method usually undervalues a project for this reason, but still forms the base for currently used computer models used in calculating the value of a mining property and the rate of return for ranking with other projects.

Payout method

This is a very simple method which ranks projects according to the number of years required to recover the original investment out of cash flow from earnings. While the payout method will serve as a preliminary screening process, and is essential in cases of companies with a high cost of capital and limited cash, its results are basically inadequate as selection criteria. The simple knowledge of how long it takes to recover the initial investment does not contribute anything about the earning power or economic life. It is usually the earnings after payout that determine whether an investment is profitable. Consider the example in Table 3.2.

It is evident that projects Y and Z achieve payout prior to project X

TABLE 3.2

	Year	Project X	Project Y	Project Z
		$	$	$
Investment	0	500	500	500
Cash flow	1	50	30	100
Cash flow	2	50	70	200
Cash flow	3	150	150	200
Cash flow	4	150	250	150
Cash flow	5	200	150	50
Cash flow	6	200	150	50
Cash flow	7–10	800	50	50
Total cash flow		1 600	850	800
Payout period		4.5 years	4 years	3 years

but that other very critical factors exist when the projects are compared. The payout method fails to consider earnings after payout and does not recognize the time value of money. The only defence for the payout method is that it plays an important role in evaluating risk where time is a critical factor. In areas of political instability where the recovery of the investment within a short time period is essential, project Z would undoubtedly take precedence over project X.

Accounting rate of return
This method is related to conventional accounting methods and computes the rate of return as a ratio of average earnings to the net and/or average project investment as shown in Table 3.3.

The accounting rate of return method is superior to the payout method because it takes into account the entire economic life of the project. It is readily seen, however, that it does not take into account the earnings trend or the time factor of money. It is clear from the example that project Y is superior simply because the same income is earned sooner. The earnings trend cannot be ignored in an evaluation of economic worth because the interest factor or cost of money must be considered as a critical component in the exercise.

Discounting
The concept of the time value of money is simply the measurement of a rate of return based on investment, earnings and time. Consider the example in Table 3.4.

TABLE 3.3

		Project X	Project Y
Investment		$500	$500
Project life		5 years	5 years
	Year	$	$
Cash flow	1	100	300
	2	150	250
	3	200	200
	4	250	150
	5	300	100
		1 000	1 000
Average cash flow		200	200
Less non-cash charges (depreciation and amortization)		100	100
Average net income		100	100

Accounting rate of return for both projects

$$\frac{\text{Average net income}}{\text{Average investment}} = \frac{100}{250} = 40\%$$

$$\frac{\text{Average net income}}{\text{Net investment}} = \frac{100}{500} = 20\%$$

TABLE 3.4

Year	Investment balance	Repayment 10% Interest	Repayment Principal	Repayment Total	Factor 10%	Present value of total repayment	Discount
	$	$	$	$		$	$
1	1 000.00	100.00	163.80	263.80	0.909	239.80	24.00
2	836.20	83.60	180.20	263.80	0.826	218.00	45.80
3	656.00	65.60	198.20	263.80	0.751	198.20	65.60
4	457.80	45.80	218.00	263.80	0.683	180.20	83.60
5	239.80	24.00	239.80	263.80	0.621	163.80	100.00
		319.00	1 000.00	1 319.00		1 000.00	319.00

It can be seen that the present value figures are in fact the reciprocals of the principal repayment amounts. To simplify, consider the value of $1 today versus the value of $1 one year from now. At 10% the $1 would grow to $1.10 in one year and to $1.21 in two years. It can be seen that at a 10% discount rate the present value of $1.21 receivable in two years is $1 and the present value of $1.10 receivable in one year is $1. This is because money earns interest. Discounting is the measurement of value after taking into account interest at a specific rate over a specific period of time. With projects costing and returning multi-millions of dollars it is clear that management cannot ignore the time value of money.

Discounted cash flow return on investment (DCF/ROI)

This might more appropriately be termed 'Time adjusted rate of return'. It is the determination of the interest rate that will discount the future earnings of a project to a present value which equals the project investment. The interest rate determined is the DCF return on the investment. The cash flows are usually discounted taking into account all complex realities of a project with the use of a computer program for this purpose. The DCF return is used for the screening and ranking of alternative projects. The following example illustrates that the DCF return is 12% on a project requiring a $10 000 investment having a life of five years with a cash flow as shown in Table 3.5. Obviously a series of calculations will have to be made in order to arrive at the DCF rate which will produce the return of the exact amount of the investment within the project life, which is why a computer is needed.

TABLE 3.5
Discounted cash flow return on investment

Year	Net annual cash flow ($)	8% ($)	10% ($)	12% ($)	15% ($)
0	(10 000)	—	—	—	—
1	2 000	1 852	1 818	1 786	1 739
2	2 000	1 715	1 653	1 594	1 512
3	4 000	3 175	3 005	2 847	2 630
4	5 000	3 675	3 415	3 178	2 859
5	1 000	681	621	567	497
		11 098	10 512	9 972	9 237

Net present value (NPV)

The NPV method is similar to the DCF method. It is based on the determination of the net present value of the project cash flow (including the original investment) by discounting the annual flow at a specified interest rate. The accounting rate of return (ROR) method ranked projects X and Y in the previous example as equal but failed to take into account the time value of money. The example in Table 3.6 uses discounting on the NPV basis, and it becomes clear that project Y is superior. The reason is simply that the same return is realized sooner and the value of having these funds is included in the NPV calculation. The selection of an appropriate rate of interest is essential in the application of NPV as a project selection technique, since the interest rate selected will be used to discount the cash flow and determine the net present value of the project. The minimum rate which should be used for discounting is the minimum required rate of return which would be the rate equal to the cost of capital for the project. However, the project cash flow is usually discounted at the desired rate of return which will be higher than the cost of capital rate. In establishing a desired rate mine management should consider qualitative and quantitative risk factors of the project. Market conditions, tax environment, political stability, pay-back period, etc., may lead management to the conclusion that the desired rate need only be 5% higher than cost of capital or, conversely, must be 10–15% more than cost of capital.

TABLE 3.6

Net present value

	Project X		Project Y	
Year	Net annual cash flow ($)	NPV at 10% ($)	Net annual cash flow ($)	NPV at 10% ($)
0	(500)	(500)	(500)	(500)
1	100	91	300	273
2	150	124	250	207
3	200	150	200	150
4	250	171	150	102
5	300	186	100	62
		222		294

TABLE 3.7

Year	Project A ($)	Project B ($)	Project C ($)	Project D ($)
0	(2 225)	(2 225)	(2 225)	(2 225)
1	1 000	2 000	500	0
2	1 000	1 000	500	500
3	1 000	500	1 000	1 000
4	1 000	500	2 000	3 343
Cumulative return	1 775	1 775	1 775	2 618
DCF return rate	28%	40%	21%	24%
NPV of project assuming a desired rate of return of 10%	$944	$1 136	$760	$1 222

Net present value (NPV) vs. discounted cash flow return on investment (DCF/ROI)

It is appropriate to illustrate a comparison of the DCF/ROI method with the NPV method to show that they do not necessarily lead to similar conclusions. Assume an interest factor of 10% in Table 3.7. It has been said that NPV provides a conservative ranking of projects compared with DCF. The NPV method requires management to specify the desired rate of return and will indicate the excess or deficiency in cash flow. The DCF will give the project's rate of return. It does not consider the desired rate of return.

There is no method of assessing project profitability which provides an absolute or perfect guide to project selection. The best method will depend on the objectives of mine management which must be consistent with corporate objectives and financial capabilities. The ultimate effect on the corporate earnings will of course almost always play a major role in management's decision. NPV and DCF/ROI methods are two of the profitability criteria in popular use; they are both important management tools. This does not mean that other project ranking criteria should be ignored. Good mine management should use every method available and remain aware of their inherent strengths and weaknesses.

Earnings per share

A shareholder is usually more interested in the return on his own investment than in the return realized by the company on its investment. Corporate earnings per share has become one of the primary factors in investment evaluation since it is one of the key determinants of the ability of the company to pay dividends. Mine management has also come to recognize the importance of the contribution to earnings per share as a measurement tool in project evaluation. The division of project income (calculated on an accounting basis) by the outstanding common shares of capital stock (weighted average, if applicable) easily produces the project contribution and is often the most important indicator of the worth of an investment. Great caution should be exercised, however, if weight is to be given to the impact on earnings per share from projects having relatively short life (1–5 years). Consideration of anything other than a long-term project will almost certainly produce an unsound criterion for project evaluation unless the return is exceptionally high.

The calculation of project income on the accounting basis is subject to all manner of problems and requires a sophisticated accounting system together with a clear definition of corporate accounting policies. Mine management must be satisfied that both the system and the policies will produce data which are realistic and practical under the circumstances if these data are to be useful for project evaluation.

There are some schools of thought which question the use of accounting incomes and favour the use of cash flow or cash earnings as a more appropriate measurement. This calculation is considered imperative as an extension of the calculation of accounting income. Proper consideration must also be given to cash required for debt service. The introduction of these factors produces a significantly different situation from the calculation of income on the accrual basis.

It must be noted that while the computation of cash or accrual earnings is an objective measure, neither basis recognizes the time value of money. Project earnings in one period are given the same weight as earnings in other periods. Management must obviously also use one or more of the discounting methods to develop the total spectrum of criteria for informed evaluation.

Mine management should be aware of the relationship which exists between earnings per share, share prices and the cost of capital. While the theory does not always hold, often for inexplicable reasons, good earnings or earnings potential usually result in a satisfactory-to-high stock price. Thus not only the dividend policy but also the actual or potential capital increment in share value, are major factors in improving the investor confidence which bears strongly on the cost of corporate capital. It is for these reasons that good management cannot afford to ignore the long-run effect of project earnings on overall corporate earnings per share.

Long *vs.* short run considerations

Mine executives must consider and determine their corporate policy with respect to the general nature of desirable new projects. Recent history has shown that the opportunities for finding small, short-run, highly profitable deposits are not significantly different from the chances of finding a large, long-run, satisfactorily profitable deposit. Priority most often will be given to the long-run profitability of the corporation.

As an example compare two projects, one with a 15-year life and a 14% DCF/ROR and one with a four-year life and a 20% DCF/ROR. There are many factors which will bear on the selection of the project, but if the short-life, high DCF/ROR project is chosen management must consider the corporate opportunity at the end of the project. What is the probability of finding a series of short-life, high return deposits? The long-run profitability may be better served by selection of the long-run project in spite of the lower return.

The availability and cost of capital is often a deterrent to management when viewing the larger, far more costly, long-life project. Management should not ignore the possible reduction in cost of capital which can stem from reduction of risk where a firm has a reasonably secure, long-run earnings potential based on very large ore reserves.

Projects with short lives run a serious risk with respect to violent, short-run metal price fluctuations. A one or two year depression in metal prices where a project has a five to seven year life will almost certainly eliminate a major portion of the return on investment. This is not to say that a long-run project would not feel the serious impact of depressed metal prices, but the total project opportunity may be less likely to prove an investment disaster.

In general, a short-life project has a higher unit cost of production than a long-life project. This factor in itself is a valid and particularly significant criterion in project selection. The relationship of project unit production costs to the world range of unit production costs is vital. Some theories suggest that if production costs do not bear the proper relationship to world or major producer production costs, the project should not be undertaken regardless of current and projected metal prices. This is based on the theory that in the long run major producer costs have a direct bearing on metal prices or vice versa.

Lastly, management must consider the overhead costs and problems in managing a multitude of smaller projects. With each individual factor being critical because of the short life, smaller projects often require the same management time and attention as that of a much larger project. The effective use of executive time must be considered since few people can divide their efforts effectively among a number of projects. The waste of executive time is simply an expensive loss of opportunity.

RISK EVALUATION

The recognition of risk and attitudes towards accepting it are very important in the life of a mine executive. It is management's responsibility to identify areas of risk and trace them back to the true source. The nature of the source of each element of risk will have a material bearing on the method selected to analyse its effect on a project. The basic elements of risk can almost always be traced back to people and geology.

Elements of risk

There are four basic factors which create the basic elements of risk in the evaluation of any project:

1. Ore reserves
2. Metallurgy
3. Operating costs
4. Metal prices

A complete understanding of the geology of the deposit is imperative to estimate accurately the distribution, grade and tonnage contained in reserve estimates. The history of the area, knowledge of similar deposits and formations, together with exploration and development to date, form the input factors with the final responsibility for determination resting with geologists. They must determine how sound the geological data are and whether further exploration is necessary prior to their making a reliable estimate.

The risks in metallurgy can often be traced to geological data. Mining methods involving the stockpiling of ore far in advance of milling can result in oxidation of certain metals causing significant increases in reagent costs if reasonable recovery is to be achieved. A fully autogenous mill required major modification shortly after construction when it was found that the grinding process was far from satisfactory and conventional ball mills had to be added to the process.

Failure to determine properly the autogenous quality of the ore or improper and incomplete sampling of the ore body undoubtedly was the cause of this very expensive problem. The metallurgist must be satisfied that his source data are complete and reliable.

Basically, most operating costs can be estimated with some reasonable degree of accuracy. Experience with underground and open pit operations in most parts of the world provides an accurate guide to certain basic costs. The principal factors contributing to errors in estimating operating costs are those relating to geological conditions which are difficult, if not impossible, to determine prior to actual mining. In an underground operation, rock and ground conditions are extremely difficult to determine prior to actual mining. In open pits, optimum wall slopes are difficult to design prior to experience, and in some instances wall failures have resulted in major economic problems. Other uncertainties in operating costs usually arise through the actions of people. Substantial increases in haulage vehicle maintenance costs were experienced in a large open pit operation. A study of driving habits indicated excessive gear changing and failure to change at proper times causing failure of transmissions and rear-ends. The education of drivers and placement of markers at shift points resulted in correction of the problem. The prediction of labour costs is probably the most difficult problem. What will happen when existing contracts expire? A study of recent contracts for similar operations may provide some guide to what to expect.

Metal prices are normally determined by the economic laws of supply and demand. Generally speaking metal prices are based on the world market and the world market is governed by the way the buyers and sellers see the supply and demand. Changes in supply occur with the discovery of major new deposits, cut-back or curtailment of production (as has happened in Chile and Africa), the withdrawal or re-entry of metal into world markets (China – antimony), or as a result of major prolonged labour strikes within the industry. Demand is affected by the world economy as a whole, although in recent years ecological factors have played a part as with mercury, arsenic and smelter cut-backs in Japan. Metal prices are very difficult to predict except within certain limits. As previously mentioned, long-run copper prices have maintained some relationship to major producer costs while short-run prices, as experienced in 1973–74, defy prediction. General economic conditions throughout the world bear direct influence on the fluctuations in demand. Such things as housing starts, ship construction and automobile production will affect prices.

Changes in technology also play a significant role. For example, plastic pipe and micro-wave transmission have altered demand for copper pipe and wire.

Risk analysis

After identifying the elements of risk, management must decide how risk should be taken into account in project evaluation. The overall concern must inevitably rest with the total question: Will the project produce a return which will satisfy corporate objectives? Risk can be taken into account by adjusting the discount rates or by adjusting the components of the cash flow calculation such as reserves, grades, prices and costs. As a practical matter, both factors will be taken into account. The size and complexities of risk models will require the use of a computer for efficient and accurate print-outs using a multitude of variables.

The adjustment of discount rates is probably the most common method of accounting for uncertainty in project evaluations. The degree of risk is taken into account by increasing the discount rate to some percentage which is higher than the corporate cost of capital. A determination of the cost of debt and the cost of preferred stock is simple, but determining the cost of common share equity capital is another matter. The cost of this capital is very difficult to measure and in the end must be determined by the judgement of management. In making this judgement management should view the determination as follows:

    Safe, long-term interest rate
  + Risk premium rate
  = Cost of equity rate

The circle becomes larger, for while the safe, long-term rate will be difficult enough to determine, the determination of the risk premium rate with any positive degree of accuracy is nearly impossible. How do stockholders consciously, subconsciously or unconsciously arrive at their risk premium rate? They probably do so without any complex or even simple calculation, but rather they settle on a figure that 'feels right'. From a more mathematical point of view, the risk premium might be described as the product of the relationship between some scale representing aversion to risk and the anticipated dividend growth rate. Once again the input data must be a product of management judgement. Management must take a logical and reasonable approach to the determination of the cost of equity capital. The addition of a high-risk factor to this figure, which will already contain some allowance for risk, may well result in over-discounting. It stands to reason that over-discounting will result in under-valuation, a problem which can arise when certain project evaluation methods are used. Consider the possibility of passing up a good prospect when estimated operating costs have been bumped up for safety, prices and grades have been reduced and then a 20%–25% discount rate is applied. As a final caution, a high discount rate will not necessarily offer protection in the event of a major calamity.

There are a number of different approaches to the methods of analyzing risk based on the adjustment of cash flow or its components. One approach starts with the cash flow as an equation then by a series of calculations, the value of a variable, such as metal price, is determined which will optimize the value of the dependent variable such as NPV or DCF/ROR. Another approach also starts with cash flow as an equation but calculates the effect on the NPV or DCF/ROR when a change is made in the value or amount of one of the input variables. The second method is the more popular of the two since it produces the type of information more readily recognized and manipulated by operating personnel. The first method produces an exact answer to an approximate question while the second method produces an approximate answer to an exact question. The latter method is favored.

The second method is in effect a process of sensitivity analysis and is very straightforward in its application. The input data can be accumulated and fed into a computer. Individual or multiple variables, such as price, grade, recovery, costs, interest rates, etc., can be adjusted and the analysis re-computed giving rapid answers to many critical questions.

Other forms of risk analysis must also be considered when using any evaluation method. The best singular description of these analyses is 'certainty analysis' with the significant components being derived from the theories of statistical inference and probability. The theory of statistical inference will assist in selection of the procedure for analyzing data while the probability theory will assist in the prediction of the expected or mean outcome of the event.

Assume that an investment of $100 million is expected to return $20 million annually for 10 years. The NPV of the investment at 10% is $23 million and the DCF/ROR is 15.1%. This value and return is dependent on all three input factors being correct. If the probability of

TABLE 3.8

	Minimum	Most probable	Maximum	Confidence level
Investment in $ millions	80	100	140	0.90
Return in $ million	18	20	21	0.90
Project life in years	5	10	14	0.90

each factor is only 80%, then the probability of the final result is not 80% but 51.2% (80% × 80% × 80%) or one chance in two that the results will be as anticipated. There is also one chance in two that the results will be better or worse than anticipated. The key question is to determine what degree of probability exists that the results will be worse.

There are many combinations of the three factors which will produce the expected returns. In order to calculate the probability of the expected returns it will be necessary to determine all the possible combinations of the three variables and reduce the calculation to a manageable size. Even with the use of a computer, it is necessary to use only a sample of the total population of variables and combinations. From the distribution of all possible values of the three variables, assume selection of three random samples of 100 of the total values, performed as follows:

(1) Define distribution by:
    (a) minimum value
    (b) most probable value
    (c) maximum value
    (d) confidence that true value is between the minimum and maximum
(2) Using these factors and a computer, construct a curve which will approximate, mathematically, a distribution within these limits.
(3) Generate 100 random numbers by computer and from these select a sample of 100 values for each variable. Select the sample in such a manner that the statistical parameters of the sample approximate those of the value population.

Assume the variables are defined as in Table 3.8.

Now assume one set of the 100 sample values is chosen and used to calculate the NPV and DCF/ROR (Table 3.9).

It is obvious that a seemingly minor change in the variables can alter the outlook for the project. The procedure should be carried out for the

TABLE 3.9

	Most probable case	1st sample
Investment in $ millions	100	108
Return in $ millions/year	20	18.5
Life in years	10	7
NPV @ 10% in $ millions	22.890	18
DCF/ROR	15.1%	4.76%

remaining 99 sample values so that, from the total, the characteristics in Table 3.10 may be determined.

Again with the use of a computer the frequency distribution must be determined which will be assumed as follows in Table 3.11.

The percentage probability of obtaining a zero or less NPV is 49%. It is apparent that the NPV of the project ranges from a plus of over $40 million to a minus of over $40 million. In considering the confidence levels which are the degrees of certainty, the foregoing illustrates the possible material variation and degree of uncertainty in the project outcome.

TABLE 3.10

	$ millions
Most probable NPV (mode)	22.890
Average NPV (mean)	1.020
Smallest NPV	(80.320)
Largest NPV	54.140
Range	134.460
Standard deviation	28.470

TABLE 3.11

NPV range in $ millions				
From	Up to	Frequency	Cumulative frequency	%
40 000	80 000	5	100	100
0	40 000	50	90	95
(40 000)	0	36	45	49
(80 000)	(40 000)	8	9	1
(120 000)	(80 000)	1	1	

The mine executive must realize that even with the sophisticated methods of analysis and extensive use of computers, the final decision for investment in a project will depend not only on intangibles such as stability of tax laws, currency exchange rates, etc., but also on his corporation's attitude towards risk. The final responsibility rests with the mine executive, and he must be confident that he has used fully every means available to him in the project evaluation to support his decision.

SUMMARY

Each of the subjects covered in this chapter has been the focal point of controversy and debate over the years. There is no perfect solution which can be handed to a mine executive, for, in conjunction with all the considerations dealt with here, there is no substitute for good judgement. It has been said that mine-makers are born not made, but if one could delve into the minds of the most successful, one would probably find a logical, systematic thought process taking place prior to any final decision being made.

The maze of considerations within project selection criteria, risk evaluation and other approaches not covered here are only given as tools to the mining executive. It is with these considerations in place that he will be better prepared to exercise his judgement effectively in the financial management of his organization.

4

FEASIBILITY STUDIES AND PROJECT FINANCING

It is difficult, if not impossible, to separate clearly the process of project selection and risk evaluation from the considerations related to the feasibility of a project. It also follows that at some stage of a feasibility study serious consideration must be given to the alternatives available for financing the project and selling the product. Each company will approach feasibility studies, sales and financing in its own way, reflecting management style.

The following discussion of feasibility studies, sales contracts and project financing does not attempt to deal with the many variations in style. It is simply an attempt to review some of the fundamental considerations essential to the management of any mining project which has reached this stage of development.

FEASIBILITY STUDIES

A feasibility study is a comprehensive report on geology, metallurgy, mining, marketing, and capital and operating costs prepared for the purpose of determining estimated earnings and cash flow in order to calculate the economic viability of a property under examination. Feasibility studies are prepared in varying degrees of accuracy, at various stages of exploration and development and for a variety of purposes. The degree of accuracy required will be reflected in the investment in time and money. The information produced by the study will be analyzed by financial personnel to determine project viability and then used by mine management as one of the prime components in the evaluation of overall project risk or project comparison.

A typical feasibility study table of contents might be as follows:

Foreword: location, access, labour, climate, environment
Summary: conclusion and brief reasons
Geology: deposit geology and ore reserves
Metallurgy: milling process required, grades and recoveries, ecology, etc.
Mining: development and mining plan and equipment requirements
Marketing: product uses, demand, supply, prices and markets
Capital costs: summary and detail of all preproduction and plant costs
Operating costs: personnel requirements and costs and operating cost details
Economics: financing, costs, revenues, taxes and cash flow projections
Appendices
   Mine section drawings
   Mine development plan and drawings
   Surface plant plan, drawings and construction schedule

The extent to which the plant engineering and design is in final form will depend on the corporate policy and the amount the company is prepared to spend in time and/or dollars to produce the feasibility study. Certain aspects, such as the construction critical path schedule, are discussed in the development and construction chapter.

Ultimate use

Prior to the preparation of any feasibility study it is essential to determine its ultimate use. Naturally it will be assumed that the prime objective is production and the study target is to determine whether this objective can be met. The evaluation of any project involves a series of studies ranging from preliminary reviews in early exploration stages to the final determination of whether the property will be brought into production. Each study in the series will provide a progressively increasing degree of certainty which results from the increased confidence in the input data. As more facts become known the greater will be the reliability of the study. If the project is to be financed externally, via debt or equity, the feasibility study will be the foundation for the financiers' evaluation and decision whether or not to proceed.

Consider the following levels of evaluation and the general approach to a study at each level:

1. Primary evaluation will take place when the exploration program has identified a basic ore body and preliminary reserve and grade estimates are available. Broad brush assumptions will be used regarding mining method, capital and operating costs and metal prices. All management wants to know at this point is whether there is *prima facie* evidence of economic viability prior to commitment of extensive financial resources to the next stage of exploration. There must be some level of confidence although the anticipated dollar expenditure or risk may be relatively low at this time.

2. Intermediate evaluation should take place as a continuing process throughout the middle and later stages of exploration. As more drill holes are made, as grades and reserves firm up and as metallurgy and other data are received a constant updating of the study should take place. Preliminary capital cost studies will be improved and expanded, flow sheets and equipment costs will be refined from factory estimates to preliminary and, ultimately, final drawings. The improvement of input data will improve substantially the accuracy of the estimate. The two-way flow of information will also assist management in determining the extent of additional exploration required to improve confidence levels.

3. Final evaluation (if there ever is one) will be the last of the intermediate evaluations and will be possible only when the ore body has been fully defined, the mining and plant design is complete to the preliminary stage at least, development and capital costs have been determined and operating costs and estimated revenues have been calculated. The final evaluation or study will then be ready for analysis of variables and risk which, if within the limits acceptable to the management, will result in the decision to proceed to production.

At each study level management should take great care to document the source and nature of input data. Every effort should be made to develop data of a quality which can be used in the final engineering stages. There is always the possibility that the property will not be brought to production, but what is uneconomic today may be viable some time in the future.

With the high cost of new projects there is an increasing tendency to consider the potential for expansion of existing facilities. If existing plant and related facilities have been virtually written off, the unit cost of expansion facilities may result in a new capital cost per unit write-off rate low enough to warrant the extraction of substantial tonnages of lower grade ores not previously economical to mine. In other circumstances, a higher tonnage throughput may reduce unit costs even after addition of expansion costs. It is not unusual to prepare a feasibility study for expansion, first, to determine if expansion is viable, and second, to form the basis for financing. In an expansion feasibility study many very significant input factors are known; however, the preparation exercise and related considerations will not differ materially from those decribed later in this chapter.

Feasibility preparation

The first step in the preparation of any feasibility study after preliminary evaluation is to determine and set down a very clear outline of the work to be performed, time schedules and the personnel responsible for each function. This is imperative since preparation of a study is expensive and every effort must be made to avoid errors, omissions or future misunderstandings.

After approval of the feasibility program the study may proceed. Essentially the study may be broken into its basic components— geology, metallurgy, site preparation, mining, milling, service, marketing, transportation, administration and economics. In order to achieve maximum accuracy and efficiency in the receipt, assessment and evaluation of data relating to these and related functions, some system should be established to formalize the input requirements. Input data will include at least most of the following.

Location
Country, province, nearest city, accommodation and banking facilities, political climate, tax laws, language, property taxes, types of map available, elevation, time zone, normal access routes, topography, hydrology and soil data.

Climate
Temperature, humidity, snow loads, wind forces, rainfall, permafrost, seafog, earthquake zoning, including seasonal variations where applicable.

Personnel
Local availability, productivity and efficiency, labour laws, union involvement, unions represented, paid holidays, vacation rights, severance pay, room and board, pay periods, travel time, training

facilities available locally, cost of transportation to remote areas and return fare policy, other major projects in the area present or anticipated, restrictions on overtime, restriction on import of foreign labour, required use of local labour, turnover rates and internal training facilities.

Transportation and communication

Ocean freight facilities, tides, harbour depths, concentrate handling equipment, shipping schedules and charges, railway access, loading and storage facilities, freight rates, highway routes, load limits, seasonal restrictions, clearance limits, nearest airport, scheduled flights, personnel and freight rates, charter availability, telephone and telex services and rates, mail service and timetables, plus distances and times for all facilities.

Ecology

Land reclamation, waste and sewage disposal, noise abatement, fume and dust control, landscaping, codes and standards, official testing agencies, names and addresses of responsible officials and all available data on possible or probable future requirements.

Geology

Topography, drainage, overburden, ground water, regional and local geology, geology of the deposit, dimensions, faulting, petrology, ore mineralogy, ore reserves summary, details and basis of ore reserve calculations and drill hole reports, maps and drawings of ore body.

Metallurgy

Test procedures and process description, laboratory test results and reports, grinding and flotation studies and reports, grades and recoveries, dewatering and project plant metallurgy and basic design.

Marketing

Survey of product uses, supply and demand, research for new uses, forecast of world production and demand, estimates of current prices, escalation and stability including a price range selection for calculation of projected net smelter returns.

Mining

Mine development alternatives, comparative cost estimates, ultimate plan selected, preproduction period development plan, method and costs, contractors' estimates, equipment and construction cost estimates, deferred development plan, operating development plan, development schedules, mining methods and establishment of production rates, sequence, grades, cut-off and reserves.

Capital costs
Details of capital cost estimates and basis for estimates of all phases of development through construction including breakdown among materials, equipment and labour, calculations for contingencies, escalation and preproduction interest costs.

Operating costs
Personnel requirement estimates, charts and estimated labour costs by specific duty, overtime estimates and costs, estimated absenteeism, fringe benefit costs, administration and overhead costs, plant service and material costs, mine office costs, development, drilling and other mining costs, milling costs including power and reagents, transportation costs, and, ultimately, annual operating costs per ton of production.

In order to complete some of the foregoing input requirements it will almost certainly be necessary to gather certain additional information essential to the project as a whole, as follows.

Administration and related services
Office building requirements, warehousing, plant security, insurance costs, explosive storage, domestic water supply, laboratories, dry rooms and equipment, and other service shops.

Townsite/personnel accommodation
Townsite facilities, local government participation (if any), other personnel housing, trailer parks, cookhouse, recreation facilities, parking, medical and dental services, schooling, stores, police, ambulance, and fire protection.

Fuel and utilities
Sources of water, hydrology, water tables, pipeline routing including complete topographical data, storage facilities and costs, natural gas access, cost and pressures, coal access, characteristics and cost, sources of electrical power, applicable codes, access to transmission lines, kVA available, installation and costs of lines, transformers and substations, location of utility company office and senior personnel.

Construction material, supplies and equipment

Costs and availability of steel, cement, aggregate, motors, control panels, small tools, piping, mill equipment, mining equipment, paint, water lines and pumps, tailings lines, conveyer belts, roofing, prefabricated buildings, laboratory equipment, shop equipment, construction equipment, sheet metal, insulation, heating equipment, airconditioning equipment, sub-contractors, general contractors and consultants including applicable freight, duty, import restrictions, prepayments or deposits, shipping times and ordering lead times where items are not available locally.

Operating supplies

Local availability, freight or delivery costs and times relating to fuel, oil, lubricants, reagents, office supplies, laboratory supplies, explosives, tires, equipment parts, balls and rods, major spares, cookhouse perishables, electrical parts and milling equipment.

Co-ordination and cost

It is obvious that the gathering and assembling of information necessary for completion of a feasibility study is a complex, time-consuming and expensive exercise. It requires careful organization and planning in order to co-ordinate all activities and achieve a timely completion. The costs of feasibility studies vary considerably, depending on whether they are done internally or externally and on the degree of accuracy and completeness required in plant design, ore reserves and cost estimates. Costs may run from $300 000 to several millions of dollars. It should be remembered that not only are these sunk costs but also that the dollars spent have a time value attached in terms of ultimate recovery.

Feasibility consultants

At a very early stage after approval of proceeding to feasibility, mine management will normally engage the services of a consulting engineering and design firm. As with other professional advisors, great care must be taken in ensuring that the firm selected has adequate expertise and experience with respect to the proposed operation. While the final responsibility is that of mine management, they will out of necessity be placing at least some significant aspects of the project in the consultant's hands. Since the work is a very practical matter, the consulting engineering and design firm may gather much of the data and prepare the majority of the capital cost and operating figures for use in a feasibility report. They may also be involved with metallurgists, other necessary consultants, and possibly have some involvement in the selection of the construction contractor when the project reaches that stage.

Analysis of data and completion

Once gathered and assembled, all data must be analyzed for completeness and accuracy since they will form the basis for the input in preparation of the final capital cost and operating estimates. Management must be satisfied with the accuracy and adequacy of these input data prior to initiating the final engineering process of plant design. If the data are not adequate then further drilling or other exploration may be required or pilot plant tests may have to be made. It should be remembered that the study will only be as accurate as its least accurate component with ore reserves, grade, recoveries and price being the most significant. A capital cost estimate error of $5 million may appear to be a monumental blunder but a difference of one-tenth of 1% on the average ore grade for a 20 000 ton/day copper mine can put operating results out by a similar amount for each year of operation.

The mining engineer must determine the mining method to be followed, the cut-off grades, and reserves. Production rates will be governed by many factors including the market for the product, ore reserves, maximum ore extraction rates, grades, available capital, required cash flow and milling process. It is obvious that a change in the production rate will change the size of the mill, capital costs, operating costs and revenues, and thus cash flow. The final production rate determination will evolve through a process of elimination depending on the ability to sell the product, engineering and finance and will probably involve comparison of several levels of production and mill sizes. Mine plans will be prepared, ore-to-waste ratios determined, mining methods determined and equipment studies carried out. Once the requirements are known, cost estimates for equipment, pre-mine stripping or main shafts and haulage-ways may be prepared. Personnel charts must be prepared including all ancillary requirements, wage scales determined, operating supplies and material costs calculated, indirect costs calculated and depreciation and amortization rates determined. Mining costs can now be calculated on a time or unit of production basis.

The milling and subsequent process must be established and costs determined. Basic plant design, principally plant size and type, will depend on geology, metallurgy, optimum mining rate and, last but not least, the ability to sell the product quantity produced. Product transportation, storage, and handling methods and facilities will have to be compared and evaluated. Water and power supplies must be investigated with methods and costs determined. Studies will have to be made of the possibility of upgrading concentrates into more valuable products prior to sale. Milling flow sheets will be prepared together with equipment and building specifications and costs. Ancillary equipment and facilities must be determined and costs estimated. Operating schedules and personnel charts must be prepared, salaries and wages determined, depreciation rates set, and the total milling and transportation costs per production unit determined.

Administrative buildings and costs, townsite and personnel accommodation, recreational facilities, fire protection, roads, sewers, domestic water and power and required support personnel must be considered, the requirements determined and costs estimated. Ecological factors must be taken into account for the overall mining, milling, administrative and personnel factors, and each cost centre plan reviewed to ensure resultant costs have been taken into account.

A construction schedule must be prepared indicating the proper melding of all phases of the construction operation from pre-mine development to equipment and construction material delivery times. It is from this schedule that management will determine the timing of cash required for capital and related expenditures and, if funds are borrowed, interest and stand-by costs during construction.

Once the total direct costs are determined management must take into account certain indirect costs and contingencies. Labour and material cost escalations during the construction period must be evaluated. Insurance, property and other taxes, consulting, engineering and design, debt interest, and administration costs can be significant over the two to three year construction period.

When all the data are assembled, design is completed, costs determined, and metal prices estimated, the feasibility study can be completed. From this, management will derive the basic data such as capital requirements, earnings and cash flow and may then proceed with studies to assess and evaluate the profitability and risk of their proposed new mining operation.

Feasibility economics

There are many variations on the ultimate detail and appearance of the economics section of a feasibility study, the determining factor usually being its end use. In most instances these financial studies are done on in-house computers or through computer terminals, and the end product is a single or series of computer runs. The use of in-house or time-shared computer facilities is the most practical and economical way to produce a cash flow report in a feasibility study considering the multiplicity of variables which management will certainly desire for ultimate consideration in evaluating the project. Many engineering and computer firms have prepared computer programs suitable for this purpose.

An example of a simple statement of estimated earnings and cash flow for a small underground operation is set out below in Table 4.1. In this example, the projections are for eight years, being the minimum proven reserves which would be acceptable to a financial house to raise the approximately $20 million capital required. As with most underground operations, development beyond the eight years would be deferred until several years after operations began because of the substantial cost attached to the capital employed in development beyond a reasonable period. The statement would be supported by data developed in other sections of the feasibility study. Examples of other financial schedules and summaries are contained in the Appendix.

SALES CONTRACTS

Many non-ferrous metal mines sell their products as concentrates rather than carrying the process through the smelting and refining stages. In most instances concentrate sales contracts are entered into for the purpose of establishing a reasonably certain market for the concentrate or metals produced which, in turn, facilitates financing of the project. In many cases major capital cannot be obtained without the project first having secured a market for its concentrate through a sales contract. In other cases the project capital, or a substantial portion of it, is provided by the concentrate or metals purchaser as part of, or in conjunction with, the negotiation of the sales contract. The seller's objective will be a contract of the same duration as that of the project's long-term debt. Every sales contract will contain its own peculiarities which will be the subject of management's wishes and negotiation. There are many aspects of these contracts which are common to agreements or recur frequently and it is therefore appropriate that some discussion be devoted to this subject.

Basic data

Management should gather the required basic facts and experts before negotiations begin. The facts required will include production sched-

TABLE 4.1
Statement of estimated earnings and cash flow (in $'000)

					Year ended				
	19-1	19-2	19-3	19-4	19-5	19-6	19-7	19-8	Total
Earnings									
Net concentrate sales	18 000	18 000	18 000	18 000	18 000	18 000	18 000	18 000	144 000
Production costs	12 000	12 000	12 000	12 000	12 000	12 000	12 000	12 000	96 000
Gross profit	6 000	6 000	6 000	6 000	6 000	6 000	6 000	6 000	48 000
Other costs									
Preproduction amortization	600	600	600	600	600	600	600	600	4 800
Depreciation	1 750	1 750	1 750	1 750	1 750	1 750	1 750	1 750	14 000
Total non-cash	2 350	2 350	2 350	2 350	2 350	2 350	2 350	2 350	18 800
Interest on bank loan	400	100	—	—	—	—	—	—	500
Total	2 750	2 450	2 350	2 350	2 350	2 350	2 350	2 350	19 300
Net earnings, before taxes	3 250	3 550	3 650	3 650	3 650	3 650	3 650	3 650	28 700
Taxes (including deferred)	1 625	1 775	1 825	1 825	1 825	1 825	1 825	1 825	14 350
Net earnings, before income debenture interest	1 625	1 775	1 825	1 825	1 825	1 825	1 825	1 825	14 350
Income debenture interest	1 400	1 400	1 250	800	400	—	—	—	5 250
Net earnings	225	375	575	1 025	1 425	1 825	1 825	1 825	9 100
Cash flow									
Net earnings, before income debenture interest	1 625	1 775	1 825	1 825	1 825	1 825	1 825	1 825	14 350
Add back non-cash expenses									
Preproduction and depreciation	2 350	2 350	2 350	2 350	2 350	2 350	2 350	2 350	18 800
Deferred portion of income taxes	1 625	1 775	1 825	1 825	1 825	525	—	—	9 400
Operating cash flow	5 600	5 900	6 000	6 000	6 000	4 700	4 175	4 175	42 550
Income debenture interest	1 400	1 400	1 250	800	400	—	—	—	5 250
Cash flow available to retire bank loan and income debentures	4 200	4 500	4 750	5 200	5 600	4 700	4 175	4 175	37 300

ules, volumes and concentrate specifications such as expected assays, moisture content, other and precious metal content (if any). The experts required will include the corporate lawyer, a senior financial officer, possibly a marketing agent and possibly a consulting metallurgist. Management must be in a position to satisfy the buyer concerning the quality of product and ability to deliver as and when stipulated. The buyer, or his agents, will want a sample of concentrate from the pilot plant in order to carry out his own metallurgical tests. The buyer may also want to attend at the plant before and after production starts to check assay and weighing procedures, etc. Essentially the seller must deliver a product in compliance with the specifications negotiated in the sales contract. The best contract is a contract which is good for both parties and will usually be the subject of long, hard and careful negotiation.

Contract provisions

Most concentrate sales contracts will contain provisions for at least the majority of the following:

1. Definition of terms, provisions for weights and stipulations regarding currencies.
2. Determination of metal prices, source of data and setting of date of determination, and base or floor prices (if any).
3. Detailed analysis of concentrate showing expected assays of all minor elements.
4. Provisions relating to assays, minimum and maximum, moisture content, other metal payments and penalties, time and place of measurement, and provision for umpire.
5. Agreement on local and foreign agents for the buyer and seller with provision for access and examination and attendance at ship loading and unloadings where overseas shipments are involved.
6. Specifications regarding point of sale such as aboard ship, 12-mile limit, etc., for purposes of accounting and insurance.
7. Details of shipping, methods of transport, definition of responsibility for cost, insurance, loading, unloading, demurrage, etc.
8. Specific details of provisional invoicing and final settlements including the timing, method and currency of payment, and provisions for interest on unsettled or late settled amounts stipulating dates and rates.
9. Details of smelting and refining setting out charges.

10. Provisions relating to insurance, strikes, lockouts, *force majeure*, etc.
11. Term of contract, termination provisions, excess and under production provisions, provision for arbitration.

As stated previously, a sales contract must be good for both parties. In times of strikes, labour problems, extreme inflation or depression a great deal of patience and understanding may be required. During 1972 and 1973 many Japanese smelters cut back production for ecological reasons, which was *force majeure* – many contracts were renegotiated simply because this was the only solution for both parties.

PROJECT FINANCING

It is rare if a small new mine is brought into production for less than $15 million; with the large, open-pit operations the total costs to production will often range upwards from $100 million to $200 million. Costs of these magnitudes used to be unheard of. Even today, while projects of this size are not uncommon, the total dollars involved tend to stagger the average imagination. How does a company raise this sort of capital: equity, debt or both? What will the cost be and what can the company or project afford? What security will be required and what will the repayment terms be? There are no fixed, pat answers to these questions, since each situation and each corporation will deal with its own problem in its own way. The only common factor is the process of determination or negotiation of terms, principally the cost of obtaining the required capital or debt. Many high-cost projects are carried out under some form of joint venture reducing each party's share of capital contributed. But that capital must still be provided from some source.

Project capital is usually derived from a combination of sources ranging from internal funds and external borrowings to the issue of equity or other types of shares of capital stock. Each source has a cost, which is determined in the market place, based on the supply and demand for funds and the security offered or risk involved. The market place for project funds of this nature is essentially international and thus the current Canadian, US and Eurodollar supply and demand will almost certainly dictate the range of interest rates which will prevail. The only other significant factor which will affect the interest rate will be risk, which is a matter for negotiation based on numerous factors including project feasibility, pay-back period, location of project (political and economic stability), stability of foreign currency, and the corporation's own financial position, management and history. Project financing is complex; each situation requires its own particular considerations and treatment. It is impossible to provide management with a set of rules or guidelines for project financing. It is imperative however that management understand the financing methods and alternatives available, evaluate and compare these alternatives, and enter any negotiations properly and fully prepared.

Financing costs

In order to compare and evaluate project financing alternatives knowledgeably, management must first understand the concept and cost of its own corporate capital. This cost of capital is difficult to define or measure, particularly when dealing with internal funds. Costs will vary from long-run, short-run, average and marginal. Each circumstance will differ but it is appropriate and logical that the proper cost for evaluation should be the corporate long-run marginal cost. Marginal cost should be the weighted average of long-run marginal costs of all capital employed by the corporation. The cost of preferred shares or debt does not present any particular problem in computation. The cost of equity capital including retained earnings is at least equal to the higher of the discounted cash flow/rate of return (DCF/ROR) on the best corporate project, or the return on some alternative investment opportunity which would be available, or discarded if the capital was invested in a new project. For short-run purposes, internal or equity capital has a minimum cost equal to the after-tax rate of return on long-term deposits receipts (3–5 years). The comparison of returns on investments and cost of capital should take income taxes into consideration. At the very least the factor used must be comparable. Other considerations in attempting to measure the cost of internal funds or shareholder's opportunity costs include the shareholder's attitude towards an acceptable return because of taxes on dividends, brokerage fees and possibly his own tax position. There is no single opportunity cost and hence no single cost of corporate capital. Management must utilize all measurement facilities available, keeping in mind inflationary trends, and settle on some rate which seems to satisfy the majority of conditions. For the corporation with an objective of maximizing profits, the minimum DCF/ROR, discount rate and cost of capital should be the same.

The cost of debt financing will generally depend on the market at the time of negotiation and in many instances will be attached to and fluctuate in relation to a prime rate established by a government body. Factors which will tend to increase the debt cost can usually be traced to those which indicate an increased level of risk. The level of risk will be determined by the lender and it is management's responsibility to dispel or at least minimize his fears, thereby eliminating or reducing the risk factor add-on in the cost of corporate borrowings. Risk will be measured in relation to corporate history, current corporate policies, value of security available, stability of metal prices, pay-back period, project feasibility, project location and the ability of management to convince the lender of its ability to make the project succeed.

Another indirect factor which can have a significant effect on the cost of financing is the fluctuation of foreign exchange rates. This is a two-way street, depending on which currency is gaining or losing on the other. Major declines of the Canadian dollar to the US dollar and the US dollar to the pound sterling, the German mark, and the Japanese yen in the late 1970s are cases in point. Many long-term debts are repayable in a designated foreign currency because metal or concentrate sales are to be paid for in that currency or the financing is provided by a foreign firm with whom the producer has a sales contract. The potential for loss on foreign exchange conversion affects not only the capital to be repaid in foreign dollars but also the interest. Consider, as an example, the effect of the rise in the value of the German mark to the US dollar from approximately 45¢ to approximately 54¢ in 1977–78 on a 9% interest rate: i.e. $(54/45 \times 100\% = 120\% \times 9\% = 10.8\%)$; 9% rises to an effective rate of 10.8%. The converse of this will, of course, have an opposite effect on the rate. The difficulties of speculating on foreign exchange movements are obvious; however, it is extremely important that management consider the potential advantages/disadvantages of structuring term debt to be repayable in the same currency as designated in the sales contract.

In addition to the direct and indirect costs of debt there are often special considerations asked for and given which form part of the overall financing costs. Underwriting and brokerage costs are normal in any equity issue. Share bonuses out of treasury or from vendor positions are not uncommon. Debt issues often include share bonuses, rights of conversion of debt to equity at the lender's option, or options on equity capital at some future date. These additional special considerations are part of the debt cost negotiation process and may well be useful management tools, provided the consequences of such action are properly evaluated. In borrowing from financial institutions such as a bank or group of banks it is not uncommon to face a standby fee for funds which they hold available but are not yet drawn down. The standby fees may vary from one-quarter of 1% up to 1%, usually in relation to the total amount involved and the agreed interest rate on the principal amount. Management is also cautioned to pay attention to the compounding factor which can range from monthly to annually. Compounding of interest, even semi-annually, will result in substantial interest on interest for a major project having a construction and pay-back period of eight to ten years.

Equity financing

The financing of new projects through the issue of common share equity capital is not common. The use of redeemable preference shares or redeemable preferred shares convertible to common shares at some predetermined price has enjoyed some limited popularity because of the flexibility it offers. The use of this type of financing is usually limited to situations where a parent company is financing a subsidiary with a significant minority position, where a major is involved in the financing of a smaller venture, or in instances where financing is being provided by a smelter or refinery. It is not unusual for a smaller operation starting its first mine to raise $2–7 million in common share equity capital with the balance of cost financed by borrowings.

An element of corporate equity is necessary in every venture; most producing mines of any size have this equity, while exploration companies bringing their first property into production on their own usually do not. The cost of such equity capital must be taken into account, dilution factors considered, shareholders' approval obtained, and the issue costs determined. With more and more new mines requiring larger amounts of capital to finance production, it is becoming rare to see a small corporation 'go it alone'. The usual outcome is some relationship with a major producer who will back the project for a substantial equity. In essence, equity financing is rarely practical because of cost; the majority of new projects are financed by a combination of internal funds and long-term debt.

Debt financing

Debt financing is currently the most popular and widely used method of financing a new venture to production, other than extensive use of available internal capital including cash flow from other operations. There are many sources of debt capital, many types of debt and security, and unlimited variations and combinations of each.

In the simplest of terms, debt financing has four basic components:

1. Principal amount
2. Interest rate
3. Repayment terms
4. Security

Debt is described in many ways usually depending on the type of security or repayment methods. Notes, debentures and bonds are basically written acknowledgements of debt. A mortgage is a document giving a claim on a property as security for debt. A sinking fund is a method of accumulation of funds for a prescribed debt repayment program. From these basic terms come the common descriptions of corporate debt such as 10% sinking fund debentures, 9% mortgage notes, 8% mortgage bonds, 9½% notes payable, 8% first mortgage sinking fund bonds, 9% income debentures, etc. The variations are without limit and are utilized to describe the arrangements negotiated between borrower and lender.

Debt financing is available from a variety of sources from private lenders, banks and financial institutions, private investor groups, and concentrate purchasers to other mining companies. There has been an increase in the activity of banks in lending to the mining industry, often as consortia to spread the risk where amounts are large.

The financing of foreign projects may be undertaken by banks depending on the country involved. Other facilities are available to foreign operations through the World Bank, and Canadian, US and other foreign government agencies. The Overseas Private Investment Corporation in the United States provides the US investor with insurance against specific political risk. In short, there are numerous sources of debt financing available for the right project in a foreign country. These are worthy of investigation but management should beware of the strings which may be attached.

Security for debt will take many forms depending on the size and term of the borrowing. Very large corporations may be able to borrow many millions for general corporate use, including project financing, without specific security but for short periods (1–3 years). This is less common than the normal practice of providing specific security by the pledge of all corporate assets and undertakings plus parent company guarantees where appropriate. It is sometimes possible to pledge only the assets and undertakings of a single specific project as security, thereby leaving other assets free of encumbrance and available for other purposes. This isolated security method will usually require some form of minimum guarantee as well and is increasingly popular in joint-venture project financing. In most cases the principal lender will require subrogation of all other debt and place restrictions on dividends and further capital expenditures. Loan agreements should specify these conditions and provide recourse by the borrower under predetermined conditions. In some circumstances prepayment is desirable and the agreement should contain provisions for this.

A material portion of project financing is often required for the construction of a townsite and related facilities. In Canada, the government agency, Central Mortgage and Housing Corporation (CMHC) has provided mortgage funds for these homes and facilities. In most instances conventional mortgage companies will refuse mortgages in remote areas since the security is dependent solely on the success of the mine and its ability to continue operations throughout the mortgage life. Under CMHC financing it is often possible to create less of a 'company town' atmosphere since employees can be given the opportunity to purchase their own homes.

Project financing is complex and there is no magic solution to the innumerable problems. In the end, each project will be financed by the best alternative available to management provided a proper and acceptable return is possible after accounting for financing costs.

SUMMARY

This chapter is not intended as a comprehensive discussion of how to prepare a feasibility study, how to secure a sales contract, or how to secure project financing. How these things are done is a matter of style. What it does give is an overview of some of the financial considerations of which management should have some basic understanding in order to carry out their management function more effectively in a style of their own choice.

5

PROPERTY DEVELOPMENT AND PLANT CONSTRUCTION

Approval by the Board of Directors to place a mineral property in production is probably one of the most significant and exciting decisions in the life of any mining executive. This approval will trigger a series of decisions, agreements and transactions involving costs ranging from $20 million to $150 million or more. With expenditures of this magnitude it is essential that financial reporting and controls be established together with some practical means of monitoring them.

The transition from feasibility to development and construction is not often clear cut. There are many aspects of feasibility which will flow directly into the final development and construction plan. Often plant design and specifications are virtually in their final stages, with only the detailed engineering drawings to be completed; detailed mining plans are often in final form; machinery and equipment specifications and even cost estimates are often complete. There are, however, many aspects of feasibility which must now be finalized such as financing, engineering and design drawings, selection of a contractor, completion of sales contracts, and setting up the management and administrative team. Certain matters discussed in this chapter may belong in the previous discussion of feasibility studies and vice versa. From a very practical viewpoint management will seldom place a project before the Board of Directors for approval unless financing is virtually assured and sales contracts are concluded. However, there remains much to do and the purpose of this chapter is to consider the financial aspects and controls which management must utilize if they are effectively and efficiently to bring the property into production within budget.

PRELIMINARY FINANCIAL CONSIDERATIONS

Once the decision to proceed to production has been made there are numerous aspects of the overall plan which must come into place before development and construction begin. Timetables must be reviewed and revised with resultant changes to the critical path program essential to any project of this nature. A management team must be established; engineering, design and construction contracts must be negotiated and concluded; major equipment contracts must be negotiated and delivery schedules set; the finance contract must be reached and drawdown provisions established to match cash-flow requirements; power, transportation and other infrastructure-related arrangements must be concluded and agreements signed.

Experience has shown that the final engineering and design will vary only slightly from the original concept; certainly there will be minor changes in process and layout, but rarely will the first-class plant be redesigned to the more utilitarian but adequate plant. While the concept for design is a feasibility stage decision, modifications in design to facilitate future expansion can often be incorporated into final engineering before or after final feasibility. Such modifications will not significantly change original capital cost estimates, but they will mean major potential future savings if expansion is carried out. These design changes to facilitate future expansion will be made only if ore reserves are adequate and management anticipates the possibility of increased future product demand.

It is appropriate that some discussion be devoted to a few specific preliminary management decisions which are not necessarily of a financial nature but which will have an indirect impact on corporate finance throughout the development and construction period. Engineering, design and construction contracts, finance during construction, cost controls and tune-up accounting are covered in greater detail later in this chapter. Brief discussion is included here of:

Management team
Critical path planning
Preproduction development cost/benefit
Infrastructure
The lenders' consultants

Management team

From the initial stages of the project planning, the Board of Directors will be accumulating the management team that it wants to bring the project through the planning stage to development and eventually into production. Figures 5.1 and 5.2 outline the basic requirements in two stages:

Pre-production and construction (Fig. 5.1)
Production (Fig. 5.2)

The preparation of a property for production is a complex process which involves an overlapping of management functions. Management must now plan, organize, implement, co-ordinate and control the development and construction programs to ensure steady and uninterrupted progress to achieve a simultaneous conclusion of these activities at the start of production. Management is responsible for ensuring that the entire operation goes smoothly and is completed as and when specified within budget. Plans, schedules and costs will change during the course of every project. It is the responsibility of management to anticipate and authorize these changes, and to keep abreast of potential problems.

The estimates, the timetables and the determination of the total capital required including revisions are normally the responsibility of engineers, and it is natural for them to resist accounting paperwork which they see as of little benefit to them in doing their job. By the same token, accounting and administrative personnel tend to react in the opposite direction in defense of their function. The ideal relationship involves an honest effort to understand the functions, needs and problems of one another. During the process of development and construction the engineers will need up-to-date cost records; and management will need revised budgets, cost to date, estimates to complete, and total cost and deviation estimates. Accounting and administration will want to control and record the transactions. This entire process will require the understanding and co-operation of all parties which, if properly organized and managed, will result in co-ordination of their respective functions and provide management with the desired results.

Critical path planning

The process by which a project with various parts flows from the final feasibility stage through development to an operational situation is organized and controlled with the help of a technique called critical path analysis. Control over the costs of each component part within this critical path is monitored by means of budgets which will be discussed later.

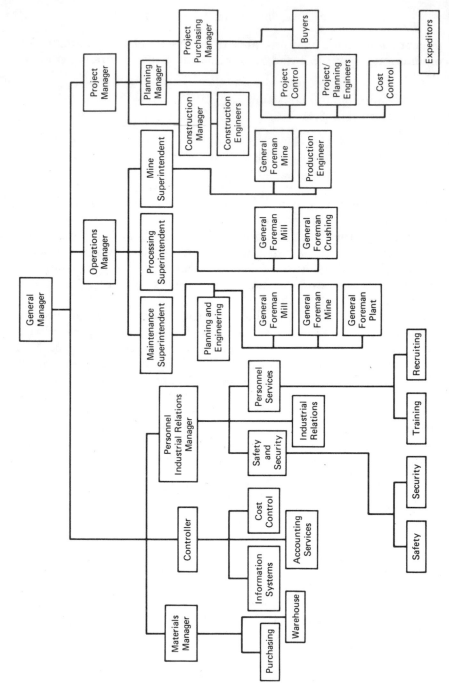

Figure 5.1 Typical organization chart for mine in the latter part of its

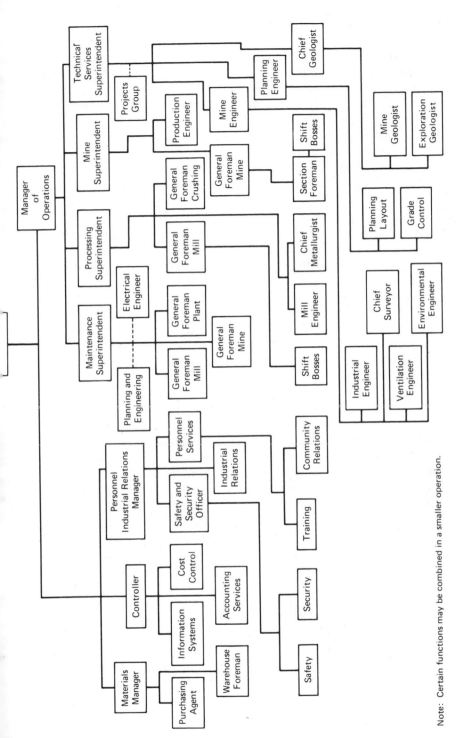

Note: Certain functions may be combined in a smaller operation.

Figure 5.2 Typical organization chart of a producing mine.

The critical path schedule will have been determined on a preliminary basis as part of the feasibility preparation. Once the production decision is made the schedule will have to be revised to reflect actual target dates incorporating contractors' timetables and equipment delivery schedules.

Critical path analysis permits the determination of that sequence of jobs which starts at the beginning of the project, ends at the completion of the project, and has no undesired overlap or free time between jobs. Each job considered here is critical in that certain sequences must be completed before the next can be started. The critical path determines the duration of the project, which is the sum of the durations of the critical jobs. When the critical path has been determined, then the non-critical jobs can be programmed. For these non-critical jobs, the job duration must be shorter than the project time and completion not critical in relation to starting times of other jobs.

Under the critical path method two time-and-cost estimates are determined for each job, normal cost estimates and crash cost estimates. Normal cost is the cost associated with finishing the job in the normal time. Crash cost is the cost associated with doing the job on a crash basis in order to minimize completion time. The basic order of approach is then:

1. Plan. Identify each job in the feasibility study and budgets; determine the latest permissible starting time for each job that will permit completion of the project in the shortest possible duration considering the desirable mix of normal and crash cost estimates; determine those jobs for which the earliest and latest permissible starting times are the same, and which are, therefore, critical jobs; determine the sequence and interdependence of jobs.
2. Analyze and schedule. The critical path can be identified and the overall duration of the project determined. The value of crashing any job can be estimated; resources, including manpower and contractors, can be determined and scheduled and the starting dates confirmed.
3. Control. Direction and control must be instituted to ensure that the permissible job completion dates and budgets are met. When cost-to-budget analysis of a project becomes complicated because the project extends over a long period of time, frequent statements showing the status of the project are required; a computer system is likely to be more practical than a manual system for recording such data and producing appropriate reports in a timely manner.

Figure 5.3 is an example of a critical path analysis used in a construction schedule.

It should be emphasized that the critical path concept can be applied to many practical situations, and useful additional information such as manpower requirements, equipment lead time and resource allocation during the development stage may be extracted from the analysis. In summary, critical path analysis helps avoid unnecessary complications and simplifies project planning and scheduling by enabling management to plan a project before any physical work is started. The critical path to be adopted should be tailored to the particular situation. It will be a combination of many variables blended together to achieve the desired plan of attack.

Preproduction development cost/benefit

Before discussing some examples of cost/benefit decisions it is appropriate to review the concept of cost versus benefit in financial terms. Regardless of the source of funds (internally generated, equity or debt) a dollar has a time cost. The earlier funds are expended in a project, the greater the time cost.

It is clearly acknowledged that there may be little latitude allowed mine management in the extent of the mine development program. The extent of exploration/development for feasibility study preparation will depend on the complexity of the ore body, the metallurgy and, in the final analysis, the degree of risk which management is prepared to accept that the information on reserves, grades, metallurgy and the mining plan is accurate and reliable.

As an example, the geological and engineering team might estimate a plus or minus 15% degree of accuracy with respect to ore body data after exploration drilling costs of $1.5 million; a plus or minus 7% after more extensive drilling costs of $2.5 million; a plus or minus 4% after sinking an exploration shaft for a cost to date of $5 million. Management must consider the cost of a 3% improvement (e.g. ± 7% versus ± 4%) in accuracy over the life of an open pit mine; in this example, interest at 10% on the $2.5 million up-front costs for a life of 12 years equals $3 million ($250 000/year), plus amortization of the additional sunk costs of $2.5 million over 12 years equals $208 000, for a total of $458 000 per year. The point here is not to suggest that management or even the prospective financier should not desire or demand a lower risk level but that the benefit must be considered in relation to its cost.

	Man weeks	19—1 April	May	June	July	Aug.	Sept.	Oct.	Nov.	Dec.	19—2 Jan.	Feb.	Mar.	April	May	June
Ramp drive and prepare 3 stopes																
Shaft house and head frame	214															T
Hoist house	228															U
Mine air	28															N
Temporary primary crusher	207															E
Ore storage and conveyors	211															
Concentrator building	503															U
Grinding	123															P
Flotation	105															
Dewatering	52															OR
Concentrator piping	426															
Concentrator electrical	72															
Instrumentation	27															R
Concentrate handling	193															U
Tailings	121															N
Site development	189															
Power distribution	103															I
Fresh water	401															N
Service building	268															
Office building	72															
Assay laboratory	44															
Ancillary building	58															
Crew size (excluding supervision)		6				139	151	143	52	34	38	42	84	96	89	15

* Based on 40 hour week

.... Sub-contract

Figure 5.3 XYZ Mining Ltd project. Critical path development and construction schedule

The same cost/benefit calculation should be considered in determining:

1. The extent of preproduction development in an underground operation
2. The preparation of a very expensive engineering and design complete feasibility study
3. The potential future savings of incorporating plant expansion plans into the initial plant design

Infrastructure

The term infrastructure is used to describe the essential support services necessary to any major mining operation including such items as power, water, roads, rail lines, airports, transportation, shipping; and such townsite facilities as homes, apartments, schools, sewage, garbage, recreation, fire, police and medical. Mines in remote areas will include most or all of the foregoing, and someone must plan and co-ordinate acquisition of these facilities and pay the very substantial costs involved.

Once again there will probably be a significant overlap between feasibility and construction; however, once the decision to proceed has been made, timetables and contracts must be completed. In addition to the technical specifications of the type and extent of infrastructure, the financing and repayment of them is a major consideration. In almost every instance there will be at least some degree of involvement of government ranging from local to regional to federal. A brief overview of only some of the considerations to the financing aspects of the infrastructure includes the following.

Power
Government or privately owned power companies will want to be satisfied that they will recover the cost of installation of service lines in addition to the cost of power consumed. Refundable deposits may be required. Contracts will have to be negotiated at a rate designed to recover installation costs and usually providing for a minimum use charge and cost escalation.

Water
The main water supply and reclaim facilities for the mill are usually a direct cost to the company and included in the feasibility financing plan. Townsite water for homes and fire protection may be financed

directly or indirectly through separate townsite mortgage or other financing means, but there will very often be some contribution and/or guarantees required from the company.

Roads, rail lines and airports
Most often these facilities will be a direct cost to the company. However, depending on location, other access and potential use, it may be possible to obtain some form of government financial participation either on a cost-sharing basis or low cost-debt. It should be remembered that government participation will almost certainly dictate public ownership of these facilities, if this is not so in any event.

Transportation and shipping
The movement of concentrate or metals from the mine site may well involve trucking, rail transport and ocean shipment. Smaller companies will almost always contract these services on a pay-as-you-go basis, as opposed to a substantial capital investment in their own facilities. Larger more complex organizations will often own their own trucking, shipping and, sometimes, rail facilities. In either case the cost/benefit calculations should be made to compare contracting, owning and leasing costs. For ownership and leasing, care should be taken to consider the management and administrative costs over and above the capital and finance costs since these are often underestimated and are the margin of difference from contract costs.

Townsite and related facilities
The cost of a townsite and related facilities is usually substantial, ranging from $2 million to $5 million plus. For this reason the amortization/depreciation period must be relatively long (20 years or more) in order to reduce the unit cost per ton mined to an acceptable level. Smaller, short-life operations may well limit housing and related facilities to a camp-style environment, comprising semi-permanent mobile home units which may be removed and sold at the end of the mine life. Larger, long-term operations will have to consider a more permanent type of operation, partly because the economics are justified and partly to retain a more stable, family-oriented work force and management team. If the location and environment are suitable many companies prefer to have the town become less of a 'company town' and encourage employees to purchase their own homes. This also encourages personnel stability. The initial financing of any

townsite will have to be arranged or borne by the company. Very often governments will participate in the financing of townsites via long-term, low-interest mortgages. If an actual village or town is formed (depending on jurisdictions) the town may arrange its own debt issues to finance capital items such as sewers, roads, street lighting, vehicles, etc. Town operating and debt costs will then be paid for via property and school taxes. It must be kept in mind that, directly or indirectly, the mine will be the principal source of funding of all capital and operating costs.

Lenders' consultants

When debt financing is used to fund all or even a portion of a new mine cost, mine management must be prepared to permit a fairly high level of involvement of mining consultants acting on behalf of the lender. Banks and other financial institutions involved to any degree in mine financing will often have staff geologists and engineers of their own. In addition, most will have working relationships with major mining consultants.

The lender will initially want an independent assessment of the feasibility study to ensure satisfaction of project viability prior to any financial commitment. This assessment may extend from repetition of metallurgical tests; consultations with in-house geologists, engineers and financial personnel; and meetings with company consultants, to extension of exploration drilling and other procedures in order to satisfy themselves that the project risk level is acceptable.

During the course of development and construction the lender will have his personnel or consultants on site at regular intervals and will almost certainly request cost to date, cost to complete, and budget comparisons on a monthly basis. In cost overrun situations the lender may also request periodic project viability update reports from the company or its consultants. In many instances the lender's consultants will have to approve the periodic loan drawdowns.

ENGINEERING, DESIGN AND CONSTRUCTION CONTRACTS

The scope and timing of engineering, design and construction contracts may vary considerably from company to company. The crucial factor is the size and capability of the in-house geological and engineering group. Nevertheless, the engagement of engineering and design consultants and construction contractors is a significant event in the late stages of the feasibility and preconstruction phases for most new mines. Since engineering and construction fees are material and because many provisions of the contracts are financially related to them, it is appropriate that some brief consideration be given here to in-house/external engineering and design, the selection of the engineer and contractor and a review of some types of contract and principal contract provisions.

In-house/external engineering and design

Virtually every mining company of any size will have some engineers on staff, with major companies often having a complete and separate engineering, design and research division. It is therefore obvious that a major company will usually do all its own engineering, design and metallurgy for a new project. Intermediate size companies may have facilities for initial engineering and design capabilities but will most often engage a consulting engineering firm for some assistance in this phase and will almost always engage consultants for final engineering and design. Smaller companies will usually engage a consultant before the start of feasibility preparation.

Selection of consultants and contractors

The selection of a consulting engineering and design firm and a construction contractor may, at first, seem to be a fairly straightforward process and indeed in some cases it is. Certainly the primary considerations will be technical competence and key personnel. However, given a selection of technically competent firms, the item of cost becomes a major consideration.

There are a variety of contract types ranging from fixed price or stipulated sum, stipulated sum plus inflation factor, cost plus fee, cost plus fee plus budget underrun bonus, fees as a percentage of cost, and a variety of combinations of these. There is an old saying that a good contract is one that is good for both parties. With a cost plus fee type of contract it is necessary to determine clearly what constitutes cost and the method of fee determination. It is also imperative that management use and closely monitor capital cost budget controls.

As with most contractors, engineering and design consultants will most often prefer their proposal to be a cost plus fee contract. Engineering and design may include just that or may extend to construction management. Internal corporate capabilities may be such that outside construction management services may not be required. On the other hand, many construction contractors have their own engineering and design facilities and these may be part of the package.

In an invitation for a proposal for engineering and design services, the technical qualifications aside, the financial considerations required should include definitions of cost and fee, schedules of reimbursable expenses and surcharges, engineering and design budgets in detail, estimated number of drawings, average and total man hours, and the estimated total cost of engineering, design, and field supervision and construction management services. Any final engineering and design contract should include provision for mine management to receive regular and timely reports from the consultant on budget changes as well as access to records for monitoring time charges and reimbursable expenses. Engineering and design costs can run to several millions of dollars and therefore require the proper degree of attention to financial control.

Construction contracts

Construction contracts normally fall into one of four categories:

1. Fixed price or stipulated sum
2. Cost plus fee
3. Unit rate
4. Cost plus fee plus underrun bonus

Since the plant construction costs will constitute the most significant portion of the total capital expenditure, it is also the area where budget overruns are most likely. For this reason the most satisfactory arrangement for management is the fixed price or stipulated sum contract. A contractor, however, will require the work to be clearly defined before entering a fixed price contract requiring a considerable amount of extra engineering and design time before the contract is signed and construction begins. Contractors are also reluctant to face the prospect of unknown cost escalations between bidding and start or over a lengthy construction period. This can be overcome by introduction of an inflation formula but unfortunately this is not always satisfactory in times of rapid inflation, since the formula itself may be difficult to define.

In the event of a cost plus fee contract there are some principles which must be followed. The fee should be a fixed amount since fees as a percentage of cost have the effect of escalating costs. In addition, the fee should be paid only at specified stages of work completion as an incentive to early and economical completion of the various project stages. Care must also be taken to ensure that a cost plus contract does not become a depository for less productive workmen, employees between projects, and the contractor's most expensive materials and equipment.

The unit rate or unit price contract is similar to a fixed-price contract. The principal difference is that the project is divided into specified units and the contractor is paid for each unit of work. Very often design will not be complete at the time of contract bidding. This type of contract will allow work to start before design completion, speeding up the work schedule. Concrete and excavation contracts are good examples of the advantages of unit rate. There are some significant disadvantages when disputes arise about what was included in unit price. Also, the full cost is not known until after a commitment is made.

A cost plus fee plus underrun bonus has some clear advantages over a simple cost plus fee contract. Essentially, the contracts are very similar in most respects except that the contractor may increase his profit by sharing in savings if the project is completed for less than budgeted cost. These savings are usually staged, as part of contract negotiation, to provide, say, a 60/40 owner/contractor sharing of savings for, say, the first $1 million underrun, then 70/30, 80/20 and 90/10 for the next plateaus. These underrun bonuses may also be set on a predetermined unit of contract basis. There may be a tendency for a contractor to cut corners or use inferior materials to make savings and here, as with other cost plus contracts, great care must be taken in preparing the detailed written equipment, material and construction specifications, either in-house or by the engineering and design consultants.

The principal features of a cost plus fee construction contract will include at least the following:

1. Project description
2. Details of the obligations of the contractor concerning:
    (a) what is to be constructed
    (b) the specifications to be adhered to
    (c) supervisory and head office costs included
    (d) date of start and target completion
3. Details of the specific definitions of cost:
    (a) salaries and wages
    (b) materials and supplies
    (c) expenditures for preparation, delivery, installation and removal of materials, plant tools and supplies
    (d) temporary offices and structures
    (e) travel expenses

(f) equipment rentals
(g) expendable materials including power and water
(h) employee benefits and other payroll costs
(i) subcontracts and holdbacks
(j) insurance premiums
(k) fees, licences, permits and royalties
(l) construction camp costs and catering
(m) updating and modifying schedules
(n) other agreed expenditures, trade discounts, etc.

4. Details of payments to the contractor for:
   (a) costs
   (b) contractor's fee
5. Provisions relating to:
   (a) general co-operation
   (b) care and diligence
   (c) undefined target estimates and modifications
   (d) where applicable, underrun bonus provisions
6. Identification of key personnel and key addresses
7. Insurance coverage requirements and responsibilities
8. General contract conditions
   (a) ownership and inspection
   (b) rejection and correction
   (c) performance bonds
   (d) warranties
   (e) termination, assignment, delays
   (f) arbitration and other related items
9. Details of work by target and bases of measurement

Needless to say, mine management is well advised to seek the advice of legal counsel with expertise in the field of construction contracts. Disputes over poorly drawn or misunderstood contracts often take years to process through the courts and the related costs can be astronomical.

FINANCIAL CO-ORDINATION DURING CONSTRUCTION

During the development and construction period, usually of two to three years depending on project size, there will be a need for co-ordination and control of all finance. This section deals with capital budget controls, cash flows and drawdowns during construction. Cost controls during construction will be discussed later in this chapter.

Capital budget controls

At the time of completion of the feasibility study the basics of the capital budget will be in place. This budget will show the total estimated cost and the estimated cash-flow requirements on a monthly basis over the development and construction period. Immediately prior to the decision to proceed to production final revisions will be made to all estimates to ensure that the project is still viable. Once the production decision is made these final estimates will form the bases for the project budget.

The project budget will represent the cornerstone for all cost control procedures during the construction period. That is not to say that the budget may not be revised as a result of modifications in design or specification during the construction period, for this happens frequently. But in order to control costs there must be a goal or a target, carefully calculated, against which actual costs and estimates to complete may be compared at frequent intervals. Variances must be explained and responsibility must be assigned. This is a control function which takes place after the expenditure is made.

Budget cost control is a method of assessing the relationship of costs to budget before the expenditure is made. It might be noted that the initial cost control is exercised in the degree of sophistication in the plant and related facility design. The plant must be designed to provide the quality consistent with good engineering. The initial project budget is based on these parameters and any subsequent changes must be carefully considered and the impact on budget assessed. The design phase has been described as being the only phase where 'creative cost control' can be exercised. The original planning of plant layout, materials to be used and avoidance of overdesign establish cost levels which cannot be readily changed by even the very best cost controls during construction.

The authority to make changes in design concepts must be carefully regulated and should rest with both a delegated senior corporate official and the designer. Changes will be made, however, and provision for regulation and control of the changes should be in place before the project starts. An Authorization For Change (AFC) or a Project Cost Change (PCC) form is a necessity and should detail the reasons for the change (technical and economic), cost details, alternatives considered, approvals, etc. This is a management tool to ensure that adequate thought is given to all changes before implementation.

Another aspect of budget cost control can be utilized in the purchase of major equipment. Where bids exceed budgeted cost and cannot be negotiated lower, management must consider the possibility of changing specifications, deferring payment, soliciting other bids, reducing transportation costs or changing the package (adding to or subtracting from the amount of the order with that supplier) in order to achieve the best possible price. Any overrun must be assessed to ensure continued viability.

The project capital budget should be designed to ensure that the various categories are broken down in such a way as to serve two purposes:

1. Budget cost control during construction
2. Plant ledger after construction

The various approaches to the use of budgets in monitoring costs are discussed at greater length under 'Cost controls during construction' but an example of the type of detail appropriate for both cost control purposes and a plant ledger after construction would be as follows:

Main cost centres for the concentrator:
 Concentrator building
 Grinding (mills, liners, conveyors, regrind, pumps, etc.)
 Flotation and production (cells, pumps, etc.)
 Concentrator piping
 Concentrator electrical (transformers, motors, controls, etc.)

Subheadings for each of the above, for example:
 Concentrator building
  Earthwork
  Concrete
  Forming
  Rebar
  Building steel
  Building finish
  Furniture

A formal budget should be prepared with a summary and total of all cost centres and, under each cost centre subheading, full details of the nature of costs to be charged. Details of component costs should be set out together with code numbers to be used for cost accounting controls once construction starts. This will ensure that future accounting accumulations of costs will be properly comparable to budgeted costs. The budget will also include provision for indirect or undistributed costs calculated during final feasibility. Examples of such costs are contractors' fees, charges and overhead, start-up costs, other consultants', engineering and design costs, construction field office salaries and expense, head office expense, interest during construction, inventory of parts and consumables, working capital and a contingency allowance.

Cash flows and drawdowns

The determination of cash flow requirements during construction is a calculated procedure based on all previous input through to the final budget. As far back as the initial feasibility the timing of cash requirements during the construction period was necessary to determine interest costs during that period. With final capital budgets in place, a final cash expenditure forecast must be established in order to budget internal cash flow and/or capital drawdowns under the financing agreement. Management of cash is very important. Premature conversion of term investments to cash will result in a loss of interest income, and a premature drawdown of external financing will increase interest expense. Some of the foregoing problems may be mitigated by good banking arrangements or the drawdown provisions of the financing agreement, but even in the best of circumstances drawdowns are usually stipulated, large round-number amounts. The effect of stand-by finance charges, and possibly compensating balances, must also be considered. Short-term investment of surplus cash will often be required in order to keep debt service costs to a minimum.

A normal pattern for cash requirements during the construction period takes the form of an 'S'-curve which would appear as in Fig. 5.4.

The cash expenditure forecast/budget will usually show that costs increase during the middle to later period of construction as major mill components are delivered and installed with related engineering and construction costs at their peak.

Proper attention to payment terms in initial stages of purchasing and to the amount and timing of contract payments and holdbacks can often have a significant effect on finance costs. For example, the deferral of payment for three months of $1 million at 15% interest will result in a saving of approximately $37 500. This is not a large amount but, if this kind of saving can be achieved several times during a multi-million dollar project, the results can be well worth the effort.

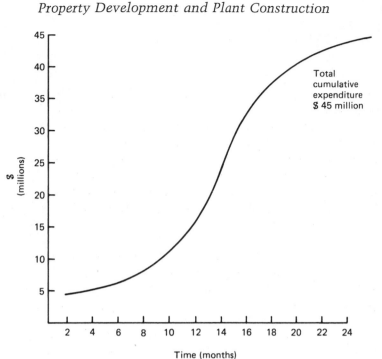

Figure 5.4 Construction cash flow requirement curve.

COST CONTROLS DURING CONSTRUCTION

At this point budget cost controls have been established, the final detailed project budget has been formalized and the construction has begun. As costs are incurred on the project there can be at least some assurance of satisfaction that they will be identified, categorized and recorded in a predetermined account. This is cost accounting which is a historical function dealing with funds expended. Budget cost controls discussed earlier dealt with costs before they were committed or expended. The historical cost data are essential for financial reporting purposes, taxation, depreciation, insurance and future projects. There is also a form of blending of budget cost control procedures and historical cost data through the course of a project which will result in a Cost Control Report which is issued, usually monthly, throughout the construction period.

Objectives of the cost control report

The objectives to be achieved through the use of Cost Control Reports and related procedures are:

1. To ensure that adequate senior management control can be maintained over the overall concept, design and scope of the project; over the commitments for expenditure of funds; and over the actual expenditures so that the project can be brought in on time and within the budget
2. To ensure the accurate recording of commitments and expenditures as they occur
3. To ensure the regular and systematic development and scrutiny of estimates to complete and to estimate final project cost both in total and in segments that are sufficiently identifiable in physical terms to monitor progress in an efficient manner
4. To facilitate early detection (and correction, if possible) of potential overruns in individual segments of the project and of the project in total
5. To provide for regular and meaningful reports to management such that they may have current data from which to control the project and to deal with related problems such as financing

It must be emphasized that a Cost Control Report will not control costs; people control costs. The report will provide information for people to make better decisions and take more timely action. If the report is not used for this purpose it has no value other than as an historical document.

Basic report form and content

The Cost Control Report will form part of a monthly reporting package to be provided for various levels of project management. The report will be a very detailed document and often senior management will receive only a special summary of the project costs indicating significant deviations from budget.

The major components of a Cost Control Report are the Cost to Budget Summary and the Cost to Budget Detail sheets for each item listed on the summary. The basic data on the summary would include:

Description of asset or asset category
Accounting code
Costs expended in current month
Costs expended to date
Costs committed

Estimated costs to complete
Projected total costs to complete
Budgeted costs
Current (over) under budget
Previous (over) under budget
Totals of each cost or budget category above

The cost centres and detail used in the Cost Control Report should be identical in detail to those included in the formal budget as discussed earlier. An example of a Cost to Budget Summary Report is shown in Table 5.1, with an example of Cost to Budget Detail shown in Table 5.2.

Related cost control procedures

During the course of construction it is necessary to control and monitor costs in relation to budget on a continuing basis. It is imperative that actual expenditures be within budget limits and, if not, that this fact be known and approved prior to any commitment. A common method of monitoring and controlling expenditures during this period is the Approval for Expenditure (AFE) forms. Every capital expenditure should be covered by an AFE. The final budget and the definitive cost estimates from which it is prepared will form the technical and cost support for the AFE.

While there should be an ever-present awareness of the possibility of achieving a cost under budget, the primary purpose of an AFE is to control costs and minimize overruns by eliminating expenditures in excess of budget unless specifically authorized. Where the AFE is within budget limits and engineering and design specifications, no other justification for the expenditure should be required. Where the AFE is in excess of budget or has to be amended, the justification for expenditure should include additional information with respect to the following:

1. Cost deviation from budget
2. Alternatives considered
3. Technical and economic evaluation
4. Basis for justification
5. Recommendation
6. Approvals of authorized person, including consulting engineer if any technical changes are proposed

AFEs will be prepared by the department requesting the expenditure and submitted to the project manager or his designate. AFEs may have

TABLE 5.1

XYZ Mines Ltd Cost to Budget Summary to July 31, 19-1

Account	Description	Expended this month $	Expended to date $	Committed $	Estimate to complete $	Projected total $	Budget $	Current (over)/under $	Previous (over)/under $
11	Pit development	5 200	1 856 620			1 856 620	1 030 000	(826 620)	(821 420)
12	Pit production equipment		11 125 600			11 125 600	10 705 000	(420 600)	(420 600)
13	Pit services, service equipment		1 149 130			1 149 130	746 000	(403 130)	(403 130)
21	Primary crusher	400	1 601 300	30 000		1 631 300	1 800 000	168 700	199 100
22	Ore stockpiling and reclaim	1 220	2 146 030			2 146 030	1 985 000	(161 030)	(159 810)
23	Concentrator building		2 713 630			2 713 630	2 758 000	44 370	44 370
24	Grinding	330	4 178 410			4 178 410	4 297 000	118 590	118 920
25	Flotation and concentrate production	8 450	1 281 100			1 281 100	1 200 000	(81 100)	(72 650)
26	Concentrator piping	1 460	467 300			467 300	420 000	(47 300)	(45 840)
27	Concentrator electrical	16 630	2 055 340	78 340	17 760	2 151 440	1 409 000	(742 440)	(629 710)
28	Tailings		3 159 030			3 159 030	2 636 000	(523 030)	(523 030)
31	Plant site development	610	1 269 800		3 840	1 273 640	960 000	(313 640)	(309 190)
32	Power distribution		1 332 890			1 332 890	854 000	(478 890)	(478 890)
33	Fresh water system		2 624 260			2 624 260	2 554 000	(70 260)	(70 260)
34	Shop-warehouse complex	50	2 283 100		100	2 283 200	2 153 000	(130 200)	(130 050)
35	Office building	100	339 340			339 340	282 000	(57 340)	(57 240)
36	Laboratory	440	432 320			432 320	348 000	(84 320)	(83 880)
37	Other buildings and facilities		166 100			166 100	82 000	(84 100)	(84 100)
38	Mobile equipment		138 890			138 890	118 000	(20 890)	(20 890)
41	Access road and outside services	700	184 990		6 400	191 390	430 000	238 610	245 710
42	Relocation of facilities		1 471 740	23 500	76 500	1 571 740	1 264 000	(307 740)	(207 740)
51	Suspense accounts	(104 930)	19 870		(19 870)			(124 800)	(124 800)
52	Contractors' overhead expenses	167 540	9 178 500	2 100	613 910	9 793 910	8 569 000	(1 224 910)	(441 960)
53	Start-up costs	170 580	2 694 970		189 710	2 884 680	1 045 000	(1 839 680)	(1 479 390)
54	Other consultants	9 280	838 650		1 000	839 650	378 000	(461 650)	(451 370)
55	Engineering and design	40	1 974 230		3 950	1 978 180	1 595 000	(383 180)	(379 190)
56	Owners' field expense	350	891 760		3 480	895 240	682 000	(213 240)	(209 410)
57	Owners' head office expense	32 190	2 649 850		190 200	2 840 050	1 065 000	(1 775 050)	(1 552 660)
58	Preproduction items	1 846 870	15 136 060	134 810	2 588 060	17 858 930	12 300 000	(5 558 930)	(989 190)
59	Contingency allowance						6 335 000	6 335 000	6 335 000
	Project totals	2 157 510	75 360 810	268 750	3 674 440	79 304 000	70 000 000	(9 304 000)	(3 203 300)

XYZ Mines Ltd Cost to Budget Detail to July 31, 19-1

TABLE 5.2

Area 21: Primary crusher

Account	Description	Expended this month $	Expended to date $	Committed $	Estimate to complete $	Projected total $	Budget $	Current (over/under) $	Previous (over/under) $
21-0100	Earthwork		144 310			144 310	145 000	690	690
21-0200	Concrete		116 940			116 940	146 000	29 060	29 060
21-0300	Forming		131 790			131 790	145 000	13 210	13 210
21-0400	Rebar		115 680			115 680	195 000	79 320	79 320
21-0500	Building steel		153 020			153 020	157 000	3 980	3 980
21-1100	Building finish		67 410			67 410	61 000	(6 410)	(6 410)
21-1200	Piping—steel	130	24 680			24 680	13 000	(11 680)	(11 550)
21-2100	Primary crusher		478 650	30 000		508 650	494 000	(14 650)	15 350
21-2200	Feeder		64 150			64 150	40 000	(24 150)	(24 150)
21-2300	Sump pump		5 270			5 270	4 000	(1 270)	(1 270)
21-3100	Overhead crane		60 250			60 250	69 000	8 750	8 750
21-4100	Rock grapple					20 000	20 000	20 000	20 000
21-5100	Chutes, hopper, liners		65 520			65 520	114 000	48 480	48 480
21-5200	Dust collection		35 120			35 120	52 000	16 880	16 880
21-6100	Instrumentation		8 000			8 000	6 000	(2 000)	(2 000)
21-6200	Misc. electrical and grounding	80	1 510			1 510	1 000	(510)	(430)
21-6300	Transformers		8 390			8 390	8 000	(390)	(390)
21-6400	Power distribution centre	190	26 930			26 930	31 000	4 070	4 260
21-6500	Motor control centre		21 810			21 810	26 000	4 190	4 190
21-6600	Motors		31 210			31 210	34 000	2 790	2 790
21-6700	Cable, cable trays		20 070			20 070	21 000	930	930
21-6800	Control panels, console		16 990			16 990	14 000	(2 990)	(2 990)
21-6900	Conduit and wire		3 600			3 600	4 000	400	400
	Area totals	400	1 601 300	30 000	0	1 631 300	1 800 000	168 700	199 100

limits for levels of authorization, and major deviations may require the approval of the Board of Directors.

Once an AFE has been approved, the department submitting it will have full authority to make commitments for the work covered by the approval. Such commitments will be in the form of purchase orders or contracts.

Where costs in excess of budget are the result of a considered and approved revision to the original design, the excess cost may be charged to a new account, the new budgeted cost being an approved appropriation from the contingency allowance. Where costs are over or under budget in the normal course of events, they will simply show as such on the Cost Control Report.

Estimates to complete

An understanding of the Cost Control Report as a management tool would not be complete without some discussion of a critical component, estimates of costs to complete each budget category. These estimates may be difficult to make, particularly in the early period of construction. Each month, prior to the issuance of the Cost Control Report, the project manager will request updates on the estimated completion cost for each phase of the project from appropriate, designated personnel. This exercise is extremely valuable in that it requires a continued awareness of cost factors in the project progress on the part of those people who have both the opportunity and responsibility to control them. Estimates to complete which indicate a final cost in excess of budget will result in immediate review and correction, if possible. It should be emphasized that the cost to complete estimates are a construction and engineering function and should be calculated on the basis of physical measure of work incomplete and facts, rather than the difference between budget and costs incurred and committed to date.

Plant and equipment ledger

The establishment of a complete, accurate and detailed plant and equipment ledger is a logical and desirable sequel to the completion of construction. There are a variety of good reasons to have such a ledger including income and property taxation, requirements for possible accelerated tax write-offs, setting internal depreciation and amortization rates, and knowledge of exact costs for equipment disposals, replacements and insurance.

In establishing a plant ledger it will be necessary to allocate many of the indirect costs accounted for separately during the construction period. These costs will include engineering and design, contractors' fees and overhead, internal overhead, interest during construction, etc. Usually these costs are allocated *pro rata* to the plant and equipment components to which they most directly relate. The concentrator, shop and buildings would, for instance, receive the major allocation of engineering and contractors' fees and internal overhead. Open pit equipment would probably bear only a *pro rata* share of interest costs. It should be pointed out that capitalization of interest during construction is restricted in the United States to those companies who fulfil the requirement of having followed this policy in the past and who have publicly disclosed this fact. The United States is currently reviewing its approach to this matter.

The segregation of all construction and equipment costs into a detailed plant ledger will normally result in four principal categories, each having appropriate, detailed subledgers:

1. Plant
2. Equipment
3. Preproduction/development
4. Supplies inventory/stores

The principles of establishing depreciation and amortization rates are discussed elsewhere.

TUNE-UP PERIOD

The tune-up or start-up period is that period of time from initial operation of the concentrator and related facilities for the production of concentrates or metals to the point at which the company considers production to be at a commercial level. Management may have some latitude in deciding what constitutes commercial production, although often commercial level will be the subject of detailed definition in finance agreements since it often triggers the start of the debt pay-back period.

In general terms, a commercial level of production is often considered to be achieved when continuous production of at least 60% of rated capacity is reached and recoveries are within acceptable limits. What term of continuous production is required varies but usually runs from 60 to 120 days, certainly a period long enough for there to be reasonable assurance that any engineering, construction and operating 'bugs' have been identified and corrected.

Change in accounting concepts

During the development and construction period all costs incurred on the project are considered to be capital in nature and therefore set aside to be depreciated or amortized as charges against future operating income. With the start of production, even in the tune-up period, the accounting methods change to those of operational accounting, the process whereby costs incurred in operations are considered to be an expense rather than capital. Once the plant is operating, all related labour, materials, supplies and overhead become an expense. Interest is no longer deferred or capitalized, and depreciation and amortization charges begin.

To prepare for production accounting, usually several months prior to tune-up, it will be necessary to establish the appropriate production and accounting reports and controls. While production reports and controls are fundamental and provide the basis for many accounting reports and controls, they will not be dealt with here since they are not a direct financial or accounting function.

The accounting for operations will require a new code of accounts to facilitate the recording and accumulating of costs and the production of meaningful operating budget and cost data and reports for mine management. A sample code of accounts for a typical, medium-sized underground operation is included in the Appendix.

New internal financial reports will have to be designed; operating budgets and control features will have to be established (these functions are dealt with in greater detail in the companion book *Mine Management*. Other new internal financial controls will have to be established to provide for proper division of duties and internal controls and checks, all to ensure accurate and proper accounting for revenues, expenses, assets, and liabilities. Stores or warehouse accounting and physical controls will have to be established (or reviewed if already in place) to ensure the maintenance of accurate stores costs and proper charge-outs for stores used in operations.

Since the tune-up period often lasts for two to three months or more, a question arises as to the treatment of operating costs and revenues during this period. In simple terms tune-up is considered a preproduction function and all revenues and expenses are accumulated for inclusion with other preproduction costs and subsequent amortization over the mine life. It should be emphasized that operational financial statements and reporting should be utilized during the tune-up period since this period will also serve as an accounting and reporting tune-up period. In addition, mine management will want to monitor costs and controls to compare with operating budget projections.

Responsibility accounting

The responsibility for the day-to-day operation of a mining project rests with the engineers, geologists and metallurgists, not accountants. The accounting function consists of the accurate, meaningful and timely reporting of all financial aspects of operations.

Accounts may be divided into past, present and future. Past represents historical costs including exploration, development, plant, equipment and preproduction together with the depreciation and amortization of these costs. Present represents all current operating costs under management control plus past costs allocated (depreciation and amortization) and certain other current costs outside the immediate control of operational management, such as interest on debt and head office overhead charges. Future represents budget projections of anticipated or target operating costs.

Responsibility accounting is based on the philosophy that management, at various levels, should be responsible for the financial results, both good and bad, of only those functions and costs for which they are responsible and can control. Responsibility accounting is a management control device and should be designed to assign responsibility through all levels of the operation on up to the general manager. The responsibility for operating results will be accepted only if operating management are intimately involved in the preparation of budgets and are satisfied that they are able to control the costs included. Operating personnel will not accept blame for results outside their control and, with respect to results in total, they must believe that they are truly part of a management team.

The accounting function for reporting the financial aspects of operations must be designed to allow a meaningful assignment of responsibility. The operating budgets and financial reports must be based on a logical structuring of principal cost centres, typical examples of which are:

Exploration
Mining
Milling
Transportation
Plant services
Administration

A summary financial report with detailed back-up data should be prepared monthly showing both current month and year-to-date figures for cost and budget with deviations from budget for both. The overall monthly operating report should contain details of and reasons for all significant deviations and corrective action taken.

Non-assignable costs such as debt interest, depreciation and amortization, and head office expense must be included to provide the complete financial results of the project. These costs should be excluded from the responsibility cost reports and included separately as an extension of the accounting function for financial reporting purposes. Operating cost reports and financial accounting reports are interrelated since the latter are an extension of the former. They should not be confused, however, since they are intended to serve two different purposes, the former cost control through assignment of responsibility and the latter overall financial reporting. An example of a responsibility cost report is contained in the Appendix.

SUMMARY

Any attempt to isolate the financial considerations from engineering, design and construction aspects of the development and construction of a new mine is at best difficult. Even the segregation of exploration and feasibility from development and construction is somewhat hypothetical since all these functions overlap as parts of the total objective.

It is not possible to set down a universal set of rules for delving through the maze of financial considerations encountered in property development and plant construction. There are different approaches in different companies and different customs from country to country. The ideas, concepts and suggestions set out in this chapter represent those in use, in part or in whole, by a variety of mining companies. They have one common thread: they are all directed towards one of management's objectives, bringing a new mining project into production within budget on an efficient and organized basis.

6

FINANCIAL ACCOUNTING

Financial accounting may best be described as the process of gathering all financial data so as to show the overall financial picture of the mining organization. These financial data are assembled to show assets, liabilities, equity and earnings to and for a specific period. The reporting form for this information is the conventional financial statement.

Financial statements are used as a management tool primarily by senior corporate officers and the Board of Directors in assessing the overall position and operating results of the company. Information provided from these statements will be of little value to the mine or mill manager in assessing his specific participation in terms of budgets, operations or cost controls. This information is, however, the kind which is required by the investor, the banker, other lenders, suppliers, regulatory bodies, taxation authorities and, last but not least, the shareholders. The financial accounting distinguishes between current assets and current liabilities to show working capital. It shows total assets, liabilities and shareholders' equity, sets out the profit or loss for the period, and indicates the earnings per share.

Financial accounting, because of its external distribution, is also the aspect of management reporting which has come under the most severe criticism by the third-party recipients of this information. The financial statements of mining companies, particularly those in the promotional stage, inevitably involve difficult problems of appropriate accounting procedure and financial disclosure. Producing mines have also been criticized for inadequate reporting, particularly as to disclosure of methods of valuation and other aspects of explanatory notes to the financial statements. Mining companies believe their accounting and reporting problems are different from other industries, which they are. However, some significant differences in the application of accounting principles still exist in the reports of some of the major mining organizations in the world. The investing public, be they individuals, institutions, creditors or shareholders, has come to place greater emphasis on financial reporting and is demanding better defined standards. These demands must be satisfied if mining companies are to retain the respect of the investing public as a whole.

The purpose of this chapter is to outline the basic concepts of mine financial accounting and reporting and to identify areas of special interest to the mining industry. With a better understanding of financial accounting and the related problems, it is hoped that management can be more effective in the discharge of these responsibilities.

FINANCIAL STATEMENTS

Basic form and content

The basic components of conventional financial statements and the disclosure of specific information in them may be governed by statute in certain jurisdictions. However, even when not governed by law, good financial reporting should include at least the following:

1. Balance Sheet or Statement of Financial Position which sets out the assets, liabilities and shareholders' equity as at a specific date
2. Earnings Statement which shows the revenues and related expenses, including income taxes and earnings per share, for a specific period ending on the balance sheet date
3. Retained Earnings Statement which shows the opening amount, adds or subtracts the operating results for the period, discloses dividends paid during the period, reflects specific material adjustments of prior periods (where permitted) and ends with the total amount retained from earnings to the date of the balance sheet
4. Statement of Changes in Financial Position or Source and Use of Working Capital (being different names for the same statement) which shows the period changes in working capital (the difference between current assets and current liabilities on the balance sheet)
5. Notes to the Financial Statements which cover accounting policies, explanations of balance sheet items and operations during the period, and other details necessary for a proper understanding of the financial statements and disclosure of material future and contingent financial matters

It should be emphasized that the corporate and other laws in the jurisdiction(s) of incorporation, including conditions of securities registration and share trading, will undoubtedly require disclosure of a variety of details relating to each of the financial statement components. Some common forms of current financial disclosure together with the wording of some of the more interesting related notes are set out with appropriate comment later in this chapter.

Purpose of financial statements

The ultimate use for which the financial statements are intended will naturally dictate the amount of detail and supporting data, particularly the notes, which will be included. Financial statements prepared for internal use and regular monthly review by the senior officers and the Board of Directors will probably include monthly and year-to-date figures together with budget and prior period comparative figures. Statements for lenders, for shareholders, and for other external use will stay more to the conventional format as shown in the examples.

The basic distinction between audited and unaudited financial statements should be clearly understood. Only when the company's external auditors have made their examination and given their written opinion on a set of financial statements can they be referred to as audited. Management should be aware of the fact that third parties such as creditors, lenders, banks, financial institutions and regulatory bodies do not always require audited financial statements. In many instances these organizations will accept interim financial statements prepared without audit on the strength of previous audited statements and on the understanding that year-end audited financial statements will be provided at a subsequent date. Unaudited interim financial statements should always be clearly marked as being 'unaudited' or 'subject to year-end audit', and management should always determine the requirements of third parties to avoid external audit costs when circumstances permit. In some jurisdictions external auditors are required to perform a limited review of interim financial statements. This matter will be discussed later in this chapter.

The attitude of modern mine management towards financial disclosure is a far cry from that of even three decades ago. The existence of larger and more complex mining organizations, all using public funds in debt or equity form, has forced mining companies to be more conscious of their public financial image. The financing of major new mines and expansion of existing operations frequently requires amounts ranging from $25 million to $200 million. Raising funds of this magnitude depends not only on the viability of a particular orebody but also on the reputation of management. It is to the financial statements that an investor will inevitably turn to assess the ability of management, through its history of success or failure.

SPECIAL MINING INDUSTRY CONCEPTS

Basic differences

As with most other industries, the mining industry throughout the world generally follows the basic accounting principles of recording assets at cost, providing for the use of these assets by charges (depreciation and amortization) to income over their useful life, providing for losses and never anticipating revenues. The concept of proper matching of expenses to revenues is also one of the fundamental principles and is probably the one area which gives rise to more problems than any other.

The mining industry in general is tending towards increased financial and other disclosure, but there is need for further disclosure in specific areas. Variations in the scope of disclosure exist in several areas. Major accounting and disclosure problems exist in the following:

1. Property location, acquisition and exploration costs
2. Property development costs
3. Financial accounting for timing differences between book and taxable income
4. Income from joint-venture and restricted foreign operations
5. Equity and joint-venture accounting disclosure
6. Ore reserves and production data

Concentrate settlements receivable

Concentrate inventories become concentrate settlements receivable when the sales contract stipulates that title passes. Settlement of balances due on concentrate shipments can take as long as eight to ten months with the normal period being approximately three months. The settlement process normally involves at least the original provisional invoice and the final invoice together with related problems concerning dates of metal prices, price fluctuations between shipment date and settlement date, moisture content and weight problems, penalties, assay differences and umpire settlements.

Many companies provide a sliding scale reserve for metal price fluctuations between the date of shipment and the price settlement date. Where the current metal price is and has been relatively stable over a period of several months on a metal, such as copper, then the reserves range from 2¢ to 4¢ per pound of metal. In a period of major fluctuation such as in 1973 when copper prices rose to $1.40 from 50¢ per pound in a period of a few months, the rapid fluctuation made necessary an offsetting reserve of up to 25¢ per pound pending final settlement. This approach is supported by the sound philosophy that the greater the risk of a significant fluctuation then the greater the reserve that should be applied, particularly in instances where the settlement date is a number of months from the shipment date.

Disclosure of concentrate settlements receivable in the financial statements is handled in numerous ways, and it is extremely difficult to state that one method takes precedence over another. As a basic premise, it is suggested that the nature and size of this item is such as to warrant separate disclosure from other accounts receivable in the current asset section of the balance sheet. Minimum disclosure should take the following form:

Concentrate settlements receivable, at
(estimated) net realizable value $2 456 789

Preferable disclosure would be to cross-reference the amount to a note to the financial statements and to explain more fully in the note the method of determining the amount, giving particular attention to disclosure of any price fluctuation reserve. If the settlements receivable is a combination of final and estimated amounts, it is desirable that the estimated amount, weight and average metal price used in the calculation be disclosed in the note.

In some instances where the sales contract stipulates a guaranteed minimum metals price, holdback provisions may be provided for a stipulated time period during and after such time as the metal price exceeds an established base. This holdback may be applied to cover the purchaser's loss if prices, as quoted by a body such as the London Metals Exchange, drop below the minimum guarantee but would be payable to the producer after a stipulated time period if not required by the purchaser to cover such losses. A holdback of this nature would usually be payable to the producer in some future year according to the terms of the agreement and, depending on the timing, would probably be classified for financial reporting purposes as a separate non-current asset. Proper disclosure would require some explanatory comment in a note to the financial statements with the balance sheet disclosure as follows:

Concentrate settlement holdbacks
(note -) $345 678

Concentrate and metal inventories

The method of valuing concentrate inventories varies between countries. In most countries of the world companies use the lower of cost or
estimated net realizable values. In Canada, provided a sales contract
exists in which the selling price is defined, it is acceptable practice to
value concentrate inventories at estimated net realizable value. This
value is obtained by the calculation of the value of metal in the concentrate, considering assays and moisture content, and deducting:

1. Freight, insurance and handling costs from the inventory location
   to the point of passage of title
2. Ocean freight and insurance
3. Treatment and smelting charges
4. Any other costs applicable under the sales contract

It is also acceptable and is becoming more general practice in Canada
to value concentrate inventories at the lower of cost or net realizable
value. This policy is considered mandatory in situations where a sales
contract does not exist. In most other parts of the world, mining
companies follow a relatively consistent policy of valuing concentrate
inventories at the lower of cost or estimated net realizable value. As an
example, net realizable value was undoubtedly the value used for at
least some molybdenum concentrate inventories during 1971 when
world prices for that metal dropped to very low levels, resulting in the
net realizable value being less than cost.

The only significant exception to the 'lower of cost or estimated net
realizable value' or 'at cost, not in excess of market' approach to the
valuation of metal or concentrate inventories, given that sales
contracts are not present, is in the case of precious metals (principally
gold) which have a relatively stable demand with no significant
treatment or marketing costs.

The term 'cost', used in relation to concentrate inventories, has a
variety of different meanings. In some circumstances the cost figure
per pound of concentrate or metals inventory would include all direct
costs but would not include such items as depreciation, amortization
of preproduction, or depletion charges on mineral properties. Many
mining companies apply the full costing or full absorption costing
concept which results in all costs being included in the inventory
calculations. Generally accepted accounting practice requires, in the

case of inventories of work in process and finished product, that cost should include the applicable share of overhead expense properly chargeable to production. Some mining companies use the 'last in – first out' (LIFO) basis, others employ the 'first in – first out' (FIFO) basis, and still others the 'average' basis. The LIFO and average bases are probably the most generally used bases in the United States with a recent trend to LIFO method in an effort to 'match more current costs of products sold with current revenues'. The LIFO method is not acceptable for income tax purposes in Canada, resulting in a predominant use of FIFO and average.

Recent studies indicate that methods adopted by the major mining companies vary from FIFO, LIFO and average with most companies using more than one method depending on the nature of the inventory. Standard costs are acceptable if adjusted at reasonable intervals to allow reflection of current conditions so that standard costs reasonably approximate costs computed on one of the recognized bases.

Mine management has come under the criticism of financial analysts in the past few years for failure to adequately disclose the principles adopted in determining the concentrate inventory amount. There is greater pressure to disclose not only the dollar amounts but also the pounds or units of each type of concentrate included in the inventory figure. While the latter information may be considered confidential to mine management, it can hardly be considered unimportant to an analyst or shareholder in his assessment of a corporation and its management. In future, greater pressures will be brought to bear, and more complete disclosure will undoubtedly result. (Refer to the section on Ore Reserves/Production Data.)

Some examples of the disclosure of concentrate inventories in the financial statements are:

	$
Concentrate inventory, at cost or net realizable value, whichever is lower (note -)	2 000 000
Concentrate inventory (for which a sales contract has been made), at estimated net realizable value	2 000 000
Concentrates, at estimated net realizable value (note 4)	2 000 000

Note 4: Under an agreement which expires December 31, 19-7, the company is

committed to sell all of the copper
concentrate produced from its DEF mill
to XYZ Smelters Ltd
Concentrates, bullion and metals sold,
in transit and on hand at estimated
net returns under sales contracts   2 000 000
Inventories, at the lower of average
cost or market   2 000 000

The use of an explanatory note is highly desirable and is used by most major mining companies in the world. The note should contain the following:

1. Disclosure of inventory by major category
2. Costing method(s) used for each category
3. Quantities of concentrate or metal by major category
4. Definition of market

It can readily be seen that the policy of valuing concentrate and metal inventories at estimated net realizable value allows the taking up of profit on that inventory in the year of production instead of the year of sale. If inventories remain relatively constant in terms of quantity and price, then only the earnings of the first and last years of operations are different, with the first year showing a higher profit and the last year a lower profit. Valuation at estimated net realizable has the advantage of eliminating distortions in earnings as a result of fortunate or unfortunate shipping schedules. On the cost basis the profit is recognized only at the time of sale. A shipment one day before year-end helps profit, one day after hurts!

It is most unusual for a mining company to place any value on products until they reach the bullion or concentrate stage. More specifically these products include broken ore, either on the surface or underground, and quantities which are constantly in the mill circuit. These products may amount to a value of many thousands of dollars, but the distortion to financial results is not as bad as it may first appear, since the initial costs of breaking ore and filling the mill circuit have usually been deferred as preproduction costs. Only under special circumstances would broken ore be inventoried with such inventory being recorded at cost. An example of such a situation would be excessive stockpiling for winter milling where winter mining is not practical. Only under these conditions will a proper matching of costs and revenues be achieved. Valuation of broken ore at cost is usually a straightforward process, but care should be taken to recognize unusual circumstances where cost may be too high a value. Experience will undoubtedly dictate in unusual cases, but one example for consideration is the excessive oxidation which takes place in certain copper ores exposed for long periods of time, which may result in much higher milling and reagent costs in order to obtain satisfactory metal recoveries.

Production payments

Some mining companies may be fortunate and enter into contracts for the present sale of future production which results in the current receipt of funds. The usual and accepted method of disclosure is to show these amounts received as a deferred revenue on the balance sheet under some appropriate description such as:

	$
Production payments	500 000
Proceeds from sale of future production	500 000
Advances on concentrate sales	500 000

It is appropriate that the nature of the production payment transaction be fully disclosed in a note to the financial statements. Such a note should indicate the general nature and term of the contract, significant dollar amounts, the method and timing of taking the deferral into income and the treatment of costs and deferred income taxes (if any) relating thereto.

Materials and supplies inventories

An operating mine must carry an adequate quantity of operating supplies throughout its life. The turnover of many items, such as major parts, extends well beyond one year with the major remaining components such as reagents, fuel, explosives and timber categorized as consumable supplies. Since there is usually not a ready market for such supplies, owing to difficult access and high freight costs, there is some logic in treating materials and supplies as similar in nature to deferred costs. It would appear that in many instances there is some argument for excluding these items from current assets. A study of the financial statements of a large number of major mining companies throughout the world indicates that this is not the case. The vast majority include materials and supplies in the category of current assets with disclosure as:

	$
Supplies, at average cost	2 500 000
Stores and materials (note 7)	2 500 000

Note 7: Stores and materials are valued
at average cost less appropriate
allowances for obsolescence
Stores – at lower of cost or replacement
cost   2 500 000

The cost of materials and supplies in inventory should include an appropriate allocation of freight costs which usually represent a material dollar value in relation to the total inventory. The inclusion of freight costs further supports the deferred cost concept of supplies inventories.

Separate disclosure of materials and supplies inventories with the basis of valuation is the accepted and usual practice, either on the balance sheet or by way of a note. Average cost appears to be the predominant method of valuation, with LIFO and FIFO used by relatively few companies. Current replacement cost data are now required in some jurisdictions and may be a required disclosure in other parts of the world in the near future. This subject is discussed further later in this chapter.

It is not entirely appropriate to state that all supplies are carried as current assets since many companies modify their policy and capitalize major mine and mill spare parts as part of fixed assets. These costs are depreciated over the estimated life of the mine on the same basis as most other major fixed assets.

Management must be aware of obsolescence which, if not realistically assessed each year, can result in significant charges to earnings in some subsequent year. Changes in basic operations or technology will render many supplies obsolete. Proper stores control with minimum/maximum levels plus systematic periodic reporting of static items will allow early recognition of these problem areas.

The last item of significance in accounting for supplies inventories is the perennial problem of minor items. Studies have shown that approximately 15%–20% of the items by unit make up from 60% to 80% of the supplies inventory dollar value. Many companies find it expedient to adopt a direct costing policy with respect to all minor items, thus eliminating a major portion of inventory cost record keeping. Stores control of these items is achieved on a unit basis only, with substantial efficiencies being noted in overall stores record keeping as a direct result. In regard to direct charges, management should be cautioned with respect to the possibility of 'hoarding' if proper stores control is not maintained.

Properties, plant and equipment

Accounting for properties, plant and equipment in a mining organization is very similar to any other type of organization with the single major exception of determination of the period of useful life. In a majority of instances the life span of a mine is extremely difficult, if not impossible, to determine. The basis for determining depreciation, amortization, and depletion rates is directly related to useful life, which in turn is related to ore reserves.

Depreciation accounting applies to tangible fixed assets, amortization accounting to intangible assets except wasting assets, and depletion accounting to wasting assets. Generally accepted accounting principles in most areas of the world require that the cost of properties, plant, and equipment be charged against earnings on some acceptable basis. The determination of an acceptable basis can be difficult but is not impossible. Conservatism usually prevails, and the write-off periods are often initially too short.

Ore reserves for open pit operations are often fairly well determined prior to commencement of operations. Underground reserves are usually proven only to the extent that the pay-back of initial capital debt can be reasonably assured. New ore bodies located close to original reserves may extend the write-off period of related facilities depending on the policy of management. Discovery of additional reserves in existing mines will also result in an adjustment to the amortization and depreciation rates with appropriate disclosure by way of note.

Probably the most significant single factor which will cause a change in ore reserves is the fluctuation in metal price. Minor price changes will in most cases be ignored. Significant price changes expected to be of a long-term nature must have an impact on the ore reserve calculation; waste becomes ore, ore becomes waste. An increase in ore reserves lowers the depreciation/amortization/depletion rate per unit and a decrease in reserves increases the rate. Management must be alert to the impact of these changes and their potential effect on the net profit of the operation.

There are a variety of acceptable methods of charging depreciation, most of which are based on units of production. Operations with a relatively constant grade may use a tons mined or milled basis while others may prefer a pounds of metal produced basis. Some of the more common methods are described in more detail in the examples which follow.

The most common forms of disclosure of properties, plant and equipment in financial statements are illustrated in the following examples:

	$
Properties, plant and equipment, less accumulated depreciation and depletion (note 5)	87 654 321
Properties, plant and equipment (note 5)	123 456 789
Less – accumulated depreciation and depletion	23 456 789
	100 000 000
Fixed assets, at cost (note 5)	
Plant, buildings and equipment	100 000 000
Less – accumulated depreciation	20 000 000
	80 000 000
Construction in progress (note 6)	2 000 000
Mining properties at cost	700 000
Less – accumulated depletion	100 000
	600 000
	82 600 000

The reference to a note in financial statements is very common, since it is by way of this note that more detail is provided. It appears logical that the disclosure in the first example above would be the preferred disclosure on the balance sheet or statement of financial position in view of the supporting data contained in the note. Significant advances have been made in the detailed information provided in the notes, some of which are required by law in certain jurisdictions and some of which are provided at the discretion of management. An example of a supporting note containing all elements of good disclosure is:

Note 5—Properties, plant and equipment ($000 omitted)

	19-2			19-1
	Cost $	Accumulated depreciation amortization and depletion $	Net $	Net $
Plant and equipment	80 000	16 000	64 000	72 000
Mobile equipment	13 000	3 400	9 600	10 800
Townsite	6 000	1 200	4 800	5 400
Roads	2 000	400	1 600	1 800
Mining properties	700	100	600	650
Construction in progress	2 000		2 000	
	103 700	21 100	82 600	90 650

Depreciation of plant and equipment is calculated and charged against earnings on a unit of production basis which, in the opinion of management, will result in these assets being fully depreciated (less estimated residual values) on the termination of their economic lives or exhaustion of the ore body, whichever occurs first.

Mining properties include only those costs of properties acquired by purchase or staking and the amounts paid under option. Depletion of properties being mined is calculated and charged against earnings on a basis identical to that used for plant and equipment. The cost of properties being explored or prepared for production will be written off on a similar basis when production begins or in full in the year that they are abandoned. Property costs consist of $100 000 in exploration; $100 000 under development; and $500 000 in production.

Construction in progress of $2 million represents costs incurred to date on an expansion of tailings facilities. Total estimated cost is $4 million, including interest during construction. No depreciation will be charged until construction is complete.

Plant and equipment costing $100 million are pledged as security for long-term debt as detailed in note X.

A number of variations occur in the above example because of poor, but acceptable, practices in certain jurisdictions. In Canada, for instance, a few mining companies in the past did not record depletion on mining properties over their economic lives but charged earnings with the entire cost in the year the ore reserves were exhausted. This and other less desirable policies will undoubtedly change over the years to conform with the generally world-wide concept of matching costs with revenues.

Capitalization policies vary from jurisdiction to jurisdiction but are for the most part consistent in that they are recording at cost, which normally would include:

1. Costs of staking or purchase of properties including purchase option payments and ascribed amounts relating to shares of capital stock issued for properties
2. Interest during construction, including interest on specific and general corporate borrowing up to the total project investment
3. All engineering, supervision and design costs
4. All related direct overhead costs
5. Major repairs and replacements only

In the United States in 1979, the recognized standard-setting organization issued a pronouncement to clarify capitalization of interest cost. The pronouncement, which has the concurrence of the Securities and Exchange Commission, permits the capitalization of interest cost for all assets that require a period of time to prepare them for their intended use. Capitalization of interest can continue only as long as these activities are in progress.

There is a growing trend throughout the world for major producers to disclose their present and future capital requirements to finance pollution abatement projects. Methods of financing and regulatory requirements are also usually disclosed. Depreciation methods vary between straight-line and unit-of-production methods with the latter being by far the more favored. Certain variations exist in the application of unit-of-production method where some companies relate the calculation to units-of-production sold. There is justification for this only if depreciation charges are not taken into account in determination of the cost of concentrate inventories or if production and other costs are deferred for matching with revenue in the period of sale.

Deferred development and preproduction

It should be noted that the word 'exploration' has been intentionally omitted from this particular topic heading. Development or preproduction costs are used here as those costs incurred after deposits of minerals or ore are considered to exist in sufficient quantity and quality to justify commercial exploitation. While these costs usually terminate at such time as commercial production is reached (after the tune-up period), it is not rare for a company to continue or begin a development program after the mine is in production. All development or preproduction costs should be deferred for amortization against related revenues. The method of deferring costs achieves the desired result of a proper matching of costs and revenues. For this method to work it must logically be assumed that there is a reasonable expectation of revenue from a project before any related costs are deferred. As mentioned in an earlier chapter, the term exploration relates to those mineral prospects which are being examined but are not yet explored to the extent that management is prepared to state that there is a reasonable degree of certainty that the property will justify commercial production. It is within this context that it is advocated that all exploration costs be charged against revenues in the years incurred, and that only development costs be deferred. If a development program subsequently proves that a property is not economically viable, the deferred development and property costs should be written off against earnings in the period during which this fact is established.

Judging when there is a 'reasonable degree of certainty' is firstly a geological and engineering matter (with respect to finding of mineral reserves to date and judgement as to their potential) and secondly an accounting matter (with respect to the potential economics in that projections, from rough calculations initially to final feasibility, must indicate a potential for profit after amortization of these deferred costs).

The geologists/engineers must establish their own basis for making the 'reasonable degree of certainty' decision and be prepared to justify this decision to the shareholders, to the Board of Directors, and to the external auditors. All recipients of this judgement must recognize that it does not constitute a guarantee or certification, but that it does constitute a considered opinion at a particular time.

Preproduction costs require little explanation, but for clarity they would generally include all development costs on a project committed to production with the exception of those costs capitalized as property, plant and equipment. Examples of preproduction costs include:

1. Pit preparation, including waste and overburden removal
2. Underground preparation, drifts, crosscuts, and stopes
3. Broken ore stockpiling
4. Interest and overhead on a *pro rata* basis
5. Financing costs on a *pro rata* basis
6. Tune-up costs less revenues earned during the tune-up period

The tune-up or run-in period of a new mine is largely dependent on the decision of operating management. The determination of the tune-up period in Canada, until the change in income tax laws in 1972, was a key issue since the end of the tune-up period was the starting point of the former three year tax exempt period. Out of this tax-based situation grew a generally accepted basis for the determination of the tune-up period and the start of commercial production. The start of production date is still of significant interest to companies throughout the world since it often triggers the start of debt repayment or royalties.As a general rule of thumb, commercial production starts and tune-up ends when:

The mine reaches a sustained production of ore sufficient to provide mill feed of at least 60% of the rated mill capacity, and
The mill is capable of processing ore on a sustained basis equal to 60% of its rated capacity, and
The mill head recoveries are consistently within 10% or less of projected average recoveries, and
The production is being sold in commercial quantities

The accumulation of deferred development and preproduction costs is generally a much simpler task than the proper determination of a method of their amortization. It is an accepted policy that deferred costs associated with minerals in place should be amortized in relation to the extraction of those minerals. Practices throughout the world indicate a strong preference for the unit-of-production method with appropriate adjustments to the amortization rates as changes are made in existing reserves. While this must be considered the preferred method, it must also be recognized that not all companies are able to determine the ultimate reserves of a mine. This problem exists more frequently in underground operations but is also found occasionally in open pit operations. The inability to prove total ultimate reserves does not justify failure to amortize deferred costs. Some reasonable basis must be determined and used until further data or experience indicates that a rate adjustment is appropriate. It must be accepted that management would not commit itself to production without some reasonable calculation of reserves to justify a return in excess of the costs of bringing the property to production. It then must hold that, even if reserves are not all proven, geological indications of probable reserves have had a significant influence on the production decision and may be used in determination of an amortization rate.

The greatest fear of management is that they will publicly overstate their expectations in relation to a particular property. The greatest criticism of both private and institutional investors is that management does not provide the basic data to allow them to make up their own minds about management's interpretation of the potential of a property. The most appropriate solution to this problem is a compromise. Management should state the basis of determining an amortization rate and be prepared to justify their decision. Rates used in Canada have varied from three years (related to the former three year tax holiday) up to an arbitrary ten or fifteen years. In other areas of the world, companies have adopted the policy of estimating mine lives and offering disclosure of this in a note, on either a specific or general basis. It must certainly be concluded that a 'best estimate' rate of amortization is far more realistic than no amortization at all.

Subsidiary companies and investments

The policy of full and fair disclosure (including that stipulated by corporate law in most jurisdictions) dictates that consolidated financial statements be presented when a corporation holds a controlling financial interest (more than a 50% voting interest), either directly or indirectly, in other companies. Exceptions to this policy exist in instances where foreign subsidiaries are restricted in respect of foreign exchange, where an unfavourable political atmosphere exists, or where control of any subsidiary is, or is likely to be, temporary.

Consolidation policies are relatively uniform throughout the world and do not present any major peculiarities in the mining industry.

Unconsolidated subsidiaries are accounted for by either of two methods, equity or cost. Under the equity method the investment is carried at original cost adjusted for the parent's share of the subsidiary's earnings or losses subsequent to the date of acquisition and for dividends received. The parent's share of earnings or losses is included in its own earnings statements. The cost method, as implied, carries the investment at original cost with income recognized only as dividends are received out of earnings from the date of acquisition. The equity method is not only the generally preferred method but also is now considered mandatory in many jurisdictions. It must be emphasized that the equity method is not a valid substitute when consolidation is otherwise appropriate.

Brief mention should be made of the accounting treatment of any purchase discrepancy, that is, the excess of the amount paid for an investment over the same percentage of shareholders' equity as stated in the investee's books at the date of acquisition. This excess over book value or premium paid can usually be attributed to calculated values (as opposed to costs) of assets of the investee (e.g. investments, mineral properties, plant, etc.). If this is the case the excess should be so allocated and written off, amortized or depreciated on the same basis as those same assets are written off by the investee company. If the premium is considered goodwill (unallocated excess), it must be amortized over a period of not less than 40 years (in most jurisdictions) or sooner if there is deemed to be a permanent impairment in value.

In the year of acquisition it is appropriate and most often required that the purchase equation or details be disclosed in a note to the financial statements. Such disclosure might look as follows:

	$
Current assets	15 000 000
Current liabilities	5 000 000
Working capital	10 000 000
Investment in associated company	700 000
Investments	700 000
Mineral properties and deferred development	1 600 000
	13 000 000
Less: Minority interest in net assets	6 000 000

Company's interest in net assets acquired	<u>7 000 000</u>
Investment at effective date of purchase:	
Cost of shares	9 000 000
Equity in earnings	3 500 000
	<u>12 500 000</u>
Excess of cost of net assets acquired attributed to mineral properties	<u>5 500 000</u>

Consolidation and equity accounting policies should be clearly stated in the notes to the financial statements. Where equity investments are material, in the aggregate, it is desirable to show summarized assets, liabilities and operating information in some appropriate form in the notes.

Equity accounting for investments

Equity accounting is often referred to as a one-line consolidation. Unlike a consolidation, the investment is carried as one amount on the balance sheet and the share of earnings or losses is shown on the earnings statement as one separate amount. The effect of equity accounting is to allow an investor having significant influence over the investee to account for his share of the investee's profits or losses as earned rather than as received as a dividend.

Certain practical and regulated guidelines have been established for the application of the equity method of accounting for an investment in which the investor is deemed to have significant influence. As a general guideline a minimum holding of 20% of the voting stock is deemed appropriate in determining when an investor, in the absence of contrary evidence, has the ability to exercise significant influence over operating and financial policies. Other factors such as representation on the Board of Directors and other opportunities to influence management must also be considered. If the investor holds less than 20% and can positively demonstrate the ability to exercise continuing significant influence over the investee, the equity method may be appropriate. The equity method of accounting should be discontinued when the investors' share of losses equals or exceeds the total carried amount of the investment, unless the investor is committed to provide continued financial support.

It should be noted that the underlying principles of equity accounting are similar to consolidation in many other respects. The company being equity accounted may follow different accounting policies from the investor; e.g. it may defer exploration costs while the investor may write off all exploration directly to earnings. The process of equity accounting requires adjustments to eliminate inter-company transactions and may require conversion of some or all of the accounting policies to those of the investor. This requirement is often forgotten in management's anxiety to control a company effectively, with the result that significant adjustment is required when the first quarterly financial statements are prepared.

Equity accounting can lead to some extremely complex accounting and financial disclosure problems. It is possible to acquire shares for performing exploration work. The investor may record the cost of this work as the cost of shares – an investment – while tax rules allow, under proper circumstances, full deduction. You then have the investor with an asset on its balance sheet which has been fully written off for tax purposes, thus creating deferred income tax. On the other hand the investee is, as permitted in Canada, carrying deferred exploration on its balance sheet which must be written off to comply with the investor's accounting policies when equity accounting! These procedures are very complicated and require complete review and analysis by the accounting department to determine the ultimate effect on the corporate financial statements. Management is well advised to make these accounting disclosure enquiries prior to taking effective control. This action may well eliminate future embarrassment and, in any event, will expose any potential problems prior to completion of the transaction.

Joint ventures

The concept and use of joint ventures has been discussed in detail in Chapter 1. However, it is appropriate that disclosure of joint venture interests from a financial reporting viewpoint be discussed here. To review briefly the concept of joint venture, it is re-emphasized that a joint venture is a 'contractual arrangement' between two or more parties (corporations or individuals) to carry out a single business venture for profit where the parties to the joint venture combine specified property, money, skill, and knowledge. A joint venture can be carried on through the medium of a corporation, in which case the objects of the joint venture are included in the incorporation documents. Other aspects of this type of joint venture will be covered by separate agreement between the corporate joint-venture investors.

While joint ventures are not a new concept, their use as an exploration or operating vehicle has increased substantially in recent years. A joint venture offers the participants significant latitude in ownership of properties and other assets, financing and tax reporting.

The original theory in accounting for a joint venture was to record the interest therein as an asset at cost, provided cost does not exceed the equity in underlying net assets. The principle here is clear in that if an item such as exploration costs is written off in the company's own accounts, there is no justification for any different treatment if such costs are incurred through a joint venture.

Investment in corporate joint ventures should be accounted for on the equity basis, as this method enables the underlying nature of their investment to be reflected. In some circumstances it may be more appropriate to use a proportionate, line-by-line basis for accounting for joint venture assets, liabilities, revenues and expenses. This method is a form of consolidation accounting.If the corporate joint venture owns all the assets and records all the liabilities, then the equity basis might be the most appropriate accounting method. If the joint venturers hold title to the assets, or their percentage of the assets, in their own name, then the proportionate, line-by-line basis of accounting may be more appropriate. This is only one of the criteria used in the equity/ proportionate consolidation decision. The nature of the joint venture, the existence of specific agreements and full details of the accounting method followed should be disclosed by way of a note to the financial statements. The note should also indicate whether the joint venture is in the exploration, development or operating stage.

In the most common form of non-corporate joint ventures the participants will contribute assets, skill and knowledge as provided in the agreement. In accounting for the assets contributed it is acceptable where possible to leave these assets combined with other corporate assets for financial reporting purposes, provided the existence and nature of the joint venture and the contribution to it are clearly described in a note. One form of disclosure is to segregate the joint venture contribution and disclose this separately on the balance sheet under the heading 'Investments'. This investment should be accounted for on the equity basis where the share of earnings and losses will be accounted for in and out of the joint-venture investment account. Both earnings and losses should be disclosed separately in the joint-venture participants' own earnings statement. This approach will result in the joint-venture investment reflecting the participants' interest on an equity basis.

Where line-by-line accounting does not take place it is both appropriate and desirable to disclose the details of the joint-venture contribution and operations in summary form in the notes to the financial statements. The extent of disclosure will be governed by the relative materiality of the assets contributed and the percentage of profit interest. This may be desirable disclosure even when line-by-line accounting takes place if joint ventures account for a significant portion of a corporation's assets, sales and profits.

An example of the balance sheet disclosure and the related note are set out below.

	19-2 $	19-1 $
Investment in and advance to joint venture (note 5)	2 000 000	1 060 000

Note 5: Investment in and advance to joint venture:

The company is a participant in a joint venture which is in the process of developing and bringing into production an antimony deposit in Australia. The benefits to be derived from the joint venture are to be shared among the joint venturers, their respective interests being 35% to others and 65% to the company. The following is a financial summary of the joint venture for the year 19-2:

Statement of financial position of the joint venture as at March 31, 19-2

	19-2 $	19-1 $
Current assets		
Cash	60 000	75 000
Accounts receivable	20 000	25 000
Prepaid expenses	20 000	5 000
Mine materials and supplies, at average cost	100 000	45 000
	200 000	150 000
Deduct		
Current liabilities		
Accounts payable	100 000	60 000
Accrued liabilities	50 000	40 000
	150 000	100 000
Working capital	50 000	50 000
Equipment and deferred development (note A)	3 000 000	1 500 000
	3 050 000	1 550 000
Deduct		
Advance from ABC Mines Ltd	50 000	150 000
Joint venture participants' equity	3 000 000	1 400 000

Equity derived from capital advance

ABC Mines Ltd (65%)	1 950 000	910 000
Others (35%)	1 050 000	490 000
	3 000 000	1 400 000

Statement of changes in financial position of the joint venture for the year ended March 31, 19-2

	19-2 $	19-1 $
Source of working capital:		
Advance from (to) ABC Mining Ltd	(100 000)	50 000
Capital advances	1 600 000	1 100 000
	1 500 000	1 150 000
Use of working capital:		
Equipment and deferred development	1 500 000	1 200 000
Increase (decrease) in working capital	Nil	(50 000)
Working capital – beginning of year	50 000	100 000
Working capital – end of year	50 000	50 000
Increase (decrease) in working capital components:		
Cash	(15 000)	40 000
Accounts receivable	(5 000)	(5 000)
Prepaid expenses	15 000	—
Mine materials and supplies	55 000	10 000
Accounts payable	(40 000)	(60 000)
Accrued liabilities	(10 000)	(35 000)
	Nil	(50 000)

Notes to joint venture financial statements for the year ended March 31, 19-2

1. The joint-venture mine development and tune-up is expected to be completed in December, 19-2 at which time commercial operations will begin. Equipment and deferred development costs will be charged against joint-venture earnings on a unit-of-production basis based on presently determined ore reserves. Components of equipment and deferred development are:

	19-2 $	19-1 $
Mine and shaft development	1 500 000	750 000
Mining equipment	1 100 000	750 000
Milling equipment	400 000	—
	3 000 000	1 500 000

2. The joint-venture participants have contributed other assets and services which remain the property of the individual participants and are not reflected in these financial statements.
3. Joint-venture operating profits or losses, as defined, are to be calculated monthly and are to be paid to or by the participants in proportion to their respective interests.
4. Each of the joint-venture participants is contingently liable for the debts of the joint venture to the extent that such liability exceeds its respective interest with the right of recovery of such excess from the others.

Deferred charges

Where material in relation to other assets, deferred charges such as start-up costs, debt discount, issue expense and development costs (when included in this category) should be detailed in a note. An example of this disclosure is as follows.

	19-2 $	19-1 $
Deferred costs and other assets (note 8)	7 400 00	7 000 000
Note 8: Deferred costs and other assets:		
Preproduction and tune-up costs	5 000 000	4 500 000
Development costs	1 000 000	1 000 000
Debt issuance expenses	600 000	700 000
Other	800 000	800 000
	7 400 000	7 000 000

Preproduction and tune-up costs relate to the Z Copper Mine which is expected to reach commercial production in July, 19-3 at which time amortization will begin. Development costs relate to the Y Zinc property which is being prepared for production in 19-4; total development costs are estimated to be $6 million. Amortization will begin when commercial production is reached. Debt issuance expenses are being amortized over the life of the related debt; amortization in 19-2 $100 000, 19-1 $75 000.

Capital stock

The more significant peculiarities relating to the issue and valuation of capital stock in the mining industry have been dealt with in Chapter 1. From an accounting viewpoint, corporate and securities laws in most areas of the world will dictate minimum disclosure requirements.

The most frequent disclosure problem arises when shares are issued for considerations other than cash. Acquisition of mineral properties and finance cost bonusing are common examples. The basic theory in the financial accounting for transactions of this kind is to record both the shares issued and assets acquired at the fair market value of the assets acquired with an appropriate note disclosure describing the 'cost' of the asset. Where shares are traded freely on a recognized stock exchange, some guidance to value is provided. In other circumstances, fair values will have to be determined by some mutually agreed process by the corporation and the recipient of the shares, with the value set out in a written agreement.

Where a cross-holding of shares exists between a parent and a subsidiary company, it is important on consolidation to disclose the number of shares of the parent held by subsidiary companies and to deduct their cost from the consolidated shareholders' equity.

Retained earnings

Once again the specific disclosure requirements relating to retained earnings are primarily dictated by corporate and securities legislation and stipulated accounting practices. Retained earnings are essentially an accumulation of annual net earnings less dividends paid. Very few other items can be properly shown as charges or credits to this account. Such items are usually referred to as 'prior period adjustments' which are specifically and directly related to business activities of prior periods, are not attributable to economic events occurring subsequent to the prior period, do not depend primarily on decisions of management and could not reasonably be estimated prior to such decisions or determinations. The most common examples of prior period adjustments include non-recurring adjustments or settlements of income taxes, settlements of claims resulting from litigation and certain changes arising from adoption of new generally accepted accounting policies (net of tax where applicable). Prior period adjustments are virtually prohibited in the United States.

The disclosure of total dividends paid should be accompanied by the amount per share for the current and comparative period. Details of material, prior period adjustments and stock dividends are best disclosed by way of a note.

Revenues and expenses

Statutory disclosure requirements for the earnings statement present relatively few problems in most countries. However, these minimum standards appear to fall somewhat short of desired disclosure if one

TABLE 6.1
Consolidated statement of earnings for the year ended September 30, 19-2

	19-2 $	19-1 $
Revenue		
Sales	60 000	25 000
Interest and other income	3 000	2 000
	63 000	27 000
Expense		
Cost of sales	30 000	12 000
Selling, general and administration	4 000	2 000
Depreciation	5 000	3 000
Amortization and depletion	1 500	500
Exploration	3 000	2 000
Research and process development	2 000	2 000
Interest on long-term debt	3 500	500
Pension and retirement	700	400
Strike costs	500	–
	50 200	22 400
Earnings before the following	12 800	4 600
Minority interest	2 000	
	10 800	4 600
Equity in earnings of associated companies (note)	10 000	9 400
Earnings before income taxes and extraordinary items	20 800	14 000
Income taxes (note):		
Current	4 000	500
Deferred	500	4 500
	4 500	5 000
Earnings before extraordinary items	16 300	9 000
Extraordinary items (note)	(3 000)	1 200
Net earnings for the year	13 300	10 200
Earnings per share:		
Before extraordinary items	$1.63	$0.90
For the year	$1.33	$1.02

The foregoing form and order of items listed is not of particular consequence; it is the content which is desirable.

takes note of the numerous criticisms which have been levelled at the mining industry by investment analysts. This section will attempt to outline the disclosure which is considered most desirable. Generally accepted accounting principles and specific statutes in the country of incorporation may dictate additional disclosure to that suggested in the example set out in Table 6.1.

Some additional comment must be made in regard to certain aspects of individual items disclosed on the earnings statement as follows.

Revenue
This is considered to be an acceptable heading and can include or show separately net sales (e.g. concentrate sales less smelting and treatment charges), interest, dividends, royalties and other revenue items. In many instances passive income such as dividends and interest may be excluded from the revenue section and shown separately elsewhere in the earnings statement. Segment reporting is considered highly desirable, mandatory in some countries, and is usually accomplished by means of a note which can segregate foreign and domestic revenues into components such as copper concentrates, iron ore, precious metals, industrial or manufacturing operations, shipping, refining, etc.

Cost of sales
This heading will normally include all direct costs of mining, milling, smelting, refining, manufacturing and shipping, etc. Where segment reporting is required or followed for revenue it is appropriate to follow suit with the related costs of sales. It is also appropriate to include depreciation, depletion and amortization in cost of sales, provided the amounts thereof are disclosed.

Extraordinary items
Extraordinary items are virtually non-existent according to accounting rules in the United States. In Canada these items are defined as gains, losses and provisions for losses which result from occurrences the underlying nature of which is not typical of the normal business activities of the enterprise, are not expected to occur regularly over a period of years, and are not considered recurring factors in the evaluation of the ordinary operations of the enterprise. Extraordinary items are not to be confused with ordinary items which are abnormal in size and result from unusual events such as bad debt losses (regardless of size), gains and losses from normal fluctuation of foreign exchange rates, and adjustments arising from changes in the estimated useful life of fixed assets. Extraordinary items should be disclosed net

of applicable income taxes and, if material, should be described in a note to the financial statements.

Changes in financial position

For a number of years regulatory bodies in various parts of the world have required that corporations include a Statement of Changes in Financial Position (Statement of Source and Use of Funds or Working Capital) with the balance sheet and earnings and retained earnings statements. The statement can be prepared by either the working capital or cash and cash equivalent method. The vast majority of mining companies interpret the term 'funds' as being working capital and in essence this statement is a summary of the sources and uses of working capital showing the increase or decrease from the previous period. This statement should begin with the income or loss before extraordinary items, with additions or deductions of income determination items which did not use (or provide) working capital. All items disclosed in this statement should be shown gross except in instances where amounts are not material, in which case netting is acceptable without using the description 'net'.

Notes to financial statements

While statutory requirements vary, most jurisdictions require that at least some minimum supplementary financial data be disclosed by way of note to the financial statements. A survey of various disclosure requirements and reporting policies throughout the world indicates that a wide variety of required and supplemental notes are used. It is apparent that the best possible disclosure would include notes on the following:

1. Significant accounting policies, which would include brief details on:
   (a) consolidation principles
   (b) equity and joint-venture accounting principles
   (c) foreign exchange
   (d) inventory valuation
   (e) capitalization
   (f) depreciation and depletion
   (g) exploration
   (h) mine development
   (i) deferred costs and amortization
   (j) income taxes
   (k) pension and retirement plans

(l) maintenance and repairs
(m) earnings per share
(n) changes in accounting policies
(o) interest expense/capitalization
2. Property, plant and equipment, showing cost, depreciation and net by principal category
3. Inventory, showing principal categories and basis of valuation
4. Investments, showing basis of valuation and market value where applicable
5. Long-term debt, including interest rates, maturity dates, security, currency and current portion
6. Capital stock, including options, issued during the year and other significant data
7. Capital or contributed surplus
8. Long-term sales contracts
9. Remuneration of directors and senior officers (if not elsewhere disclosed)
10. Commitments and contingencies
11. Income taxes
12. Pension and retirement plans
13. Other income (where material)
14. Subsequent events
15. Related party transactions
16. Extraordinary items
17. Segmented information both by industry and by geographic area
18. Other material matters

The 'accounting policies' note should be utilized only for the disclosure of policies as such. Occasionally the accounting policies are set out separately and not included with the usual notes to the financial statements. Other notes should be utilized to disclose dollar amounts and related pertinent details. It is evident from the foregoing that a great deal of detailed information will be provided if notes are included as suggested here. The greatest criticism of mining company financial statements by the public and investment analysts is the industry's failure to provide adequate detail by way of notes of this nature. There has been a significant improvement in disclosure during the 1970s.

Foreign operations and exchange gains/losses

The mining industry has many special problems in the treatment of foreign operations in their financial statements. Greater mobility and high demand for certain metals have resulted in increased foreign activity by many mining companies. With this increased use of foreign ore deposits come the uncertainties of exchange restriction, devaluation, nationalization and government regulation. In determining consolidation policies for foreign subsidiaries, all these uncertainties deserve serious consideration. Adequate disclosure of significant foreign operations should be made regardless of the accounting treatment followed. As previously advocated, foreign exchange conversion policies should be stated together with the treatment of both realized and unrealized exchange gains and losses. Policies with respect to the treatment of unrealized foreign exchange gains or losses vary rather significantly from country to country, with both Canada and the United States reconsidering their present policies. At the time of writing, in Canada, a variety of accounting methods for translating foreign currency are acceptable as long as full disclosure is provided. Perhaps the most common method is to translate current assets and liabilities at current exchange rates, and non-current assets and liabilities at the historical exchange rate. The basis of translation should be disclosed and, where the carrying value of long-term debt denominated in a foreign currency differs significantly from the amount of the debt translated at the current exchange rate, the amount of the difference should be disclosed.

In the US presently, a draft proposal for translating foreign currency financial statements encourages US companies to use the current exchange rate for all balance sheet transactions, average rates to translate revenues and expenses, and resulting transaction gains and losses to be recorded as a separate component of shareholders' equity (excluded from current earnings).

The effect of the exchange rate is considered to apply to the net investment in a foreign entity rather than to its individual assets and liabilities, and the proposal is called the functional currency approach.

Only exchange gains and losses on monetary items of foreign currency transactions would continue to be included in determining net income for the period in which exchange rates change. The UK has issued a draft proposal on foreign currency translation which is similar to the US draft.

Ore reserves/production data

At present, many financial statements do not show estimated mineral reserves recoverable, other than by way of capitalization of the mineral properties and deferral of related development costs. Financial analysts have been urging disclosure of this information for many years. The evaluation of the financial position and operating results of a mining company cannot be complete without some form of simultaneous evaluation of mineral reserves and the company's exploration policy. Production data by operation—showing tons mined and milled, ore grades, recoveries, and other similar pertinent information—are frequently shown and this is considered to be good disclosure policy. While mineral reserve and production information is not necessary on the balance sheet or in notes to the financial statements, it is highly desirable that disclosure be made in some other appropriate section of the annual report.

Complete disclosure relating to mineral reserves should include at least the following information:

1. Total reserves owned by geographical location
2. Reserves added during the year indicating whether by discovery, development, purchase or revision of estimates
3. Reserves mined during the year
4. Remaining reserves
5. Comparative data
6. Details of grades, other measurement data and economic recovery factors so as to caution the reader against attributing greater significance to the data than is warranted (e.g. define proven, probable and possible reserves)

In the United States in 1980, the recognized accounting organization which establishes and interprets standards of financial accounting and reporting issued a pronouncement requiring large mining companies to disclose, as unaudited supplementary information, estimates of significant quantities of proven, or proven and probable mineral reserves as at the end of the year or at the most recent date during the year for which estimates can be made, accompanied by comparative information for each of their preceding four fiscal years. In addition, quantities of each significant mineral produced during the year are required to be disclosed along with quantities sold and the average sales price. This pronouncement, developed out of current cost reporting on the effects of inflation, is further discussed at the conclusion of this section. Companies not required to comply with the above are encouraged to do so voluntarily.

INTERIM FINANCIAL REPORTING

The issuance of quarterly and/or semi-annual financial information to shareholders has become a legislated requirement in many parts of the world. The required content, disclosure and frequency of these reports vary from country to country, with the United States being the most stringent in its requirements.

Form and content

With the exception of certain smaller exempt corporations, the reporting requirements in the United States require the presentation of an income statement, a balance sheet and a statement of changes in financial position. Other countries do not require a balance sheet and most countries do not require the inclusion of detailed notes to the financial statements. In the United States reporting is required quarterly; in Canada, compliance with The Ontario Securities Act requires quarterly reporting. As a practical matter, many Canadian mining companies report to their shareholders on a quarterly basis.

It should be noted that interim financial information need not be audited and this fact should be clearly indicated on the statement. The United States does, however, require that selected quarterly data be disclosed in notes to annual financial statements. While this information is unaudited, there is a presumed association by the external auditor with the figures contained in the notes. The Securities and Exchange Commission presumes appropriate professional review standards have been applied by the independent public accountant who is associated with this statement. As a very practical matter, the auditors of most major mining companies perform a limited review (not an audit) on a quarterly basis prior to release of quarterly information to the shareholders.

The quarterly information required in the annual report includes at least the following on a comparative basis:

1. Net sales
2. Gross profit
3. Net income
4. Net income per common share
5. High and low stock prices

Accounting changes

Once again the United States prescribes the most stringent requirements with respect to accounting changes, both on quarterly reporting and on the annual financial statements. Their requirements include the provision that the company's independent auditor shall state whether or not the accounting change is to an alternative principle which in his judgement is preferable under the circumstances. This requirement of the auditor does not exist elsewhere.

If a change in accounting principles is made subsequent to the first quarter and not disclosed separately to shareholders, relevant disclosure of the effect on the interim periods should be made in a note to the company's annual financial statements.

Income taxes in interim periods

Brief comment is warranted on the subject of computation of income taxes for interim periods because of the complexities involved in determination of an appropriate amount. Without entering the complex technicalities of the subject, the taxes should be calculated first on a projected annual basis and then apportioned back to each quarter on essentially a *pro rata* basis. Projection updates are obviously necessary each quarter.

Special rules exist for computation of interim period taxes applicable to significant unusual items, discontinued operations, extraordinary items and cumulative effects of changes in accounting principles.

CURRENT VALUE/REPLACEMENT COST ACCOUNTING

The double-digit inflation era which started in the late 1960s and continued through the 1970s frequently resulted in very high profits in many resource based industries, including much of the mining industry. Public outcries of excess profits and other less kind terms have led many industries, the oil and gas industry also being very much involved, to consider the means of justifying and explaining these profits to which industry felt it was justly entitled. Further, a high percentage of these profits can be artificial. Out of these presumed deficiencies of the traditional historical cost basis of accounting in dealing with the impact of inflation grew many different but similar theories as to how the historical method could be improved. Current replacement cost, current cost accounting, replacement cost accounting and current value accounting are some of the better-known terms. None are new, however, since some countries have followed some form of current value accounting for decades. While each of the theories has its own basis, the essence of all is to find some way to relate historical costs to a current cost or value and, after adjustment for new depreciation and amortization amounts, to calculate a new earnings figure. In a great many cases the effect of increased depreciation charges, resulting from writing up asset costs to current values, had the effect of reducing profits, sometimes very substantially.

There still exists a great deal of controversy as to whether or not any form of current value accounting is necessary or desirable. The ultimate decision to proceed or abandon may still be years down the road.

State of the art

International

The principal international accounting standards committee has released a proposal to require large public enterprises to present information on how changing prices affect their financial results. Since there is no international consensus on which method is best, the committee believes that various methods and combinations should be experimented with and presented on a supplementary basis.

Canada

The public accounting bodies have not yet reached any consensus as to the mandatory disclosure of current value data. The present proposal, for which experimentation and comment have been requested, is for disclosure of current cost information by large publicly traded companies only, to be presented as unaudited supplementary information in annual reports. Current cost, being the amount needed to acquire an asset identical or equivalent to that owned and subject to the test of net realizable value, would be provided for inventories, property, plant and equipment, changes in shareholders' equity and earnings per share.

Canadian proposals, which are generally similar to the UK requirements, differ from the US requirements principally in that the US also requires that constant dollar (general price level) information be provided in addition to the current cost information. A number of major Canadian companies, including some mining companies, have already volunteered supplementary current value data in conjunction with their annual reports to shareholders; however, the content and format vary widely.

United States

In 1979, the recognized accounting organization which establishes and interprets standards of financial accounting and reporting issued a pronouncement requiring large publicly held companies, on an experimental basis, to make supplemental disclosures of certain effects of changing prices on their enterprises. The disclosures, required in any published report containing the annual financial statements, include measurement of certain assets and of income from continuing operations on the basis of both constant dollar (i.e. adjusted for general inflation) and current cost accounting (i.e. adjusted for changes in specific prices). Companies not required to comply with the above are encouraged to do so voluntarily.

Research and review of the methods employed in reporting are continuing and information on results by industry is being compiled and made available to users.

With the implementation of the above, the Securities and Exchange Commission deleted its own rule originating in 1976 with regard to required disclosure of current replacement cost data for large registrants.

The mining industry was exempted for the first year from the current cost disclosure requirements referred to above because there was no consensus as to the accepted approach for measuring the current finding cost of nonrenewable natural resources. In 1980, guidelines were issued in this regard which stated that current cost of mineral ore bodies and development could be estimated with acceptable reliability. Accordingly, although fair value of mineral bodies should not be presented, information on quantities and prices should be provided. (Refer also to the section on ore reserves/production data.)

United Kingdom
In 1979, new proposals were released for disclosure by certain companies of the effects of changing prices by including, in their historical cost financial statements, a current cost profit and loss statement and balance sheet as well as explanatory notes. The current cost profit and loss statement would show the current cost operating profit derived after making depreciation, cost of sales and monetary working capital adjustments and the resulting current cost profit attributable to shareholders.

Australia
Disclosure of the effects of inflation on results of operations is voluntary. Where disclosure is provided, the format is usually similar to that followed in the UK.

SUMMARY

It can readily be seen that the characteristics of the operations of the mining industry create some particularly difficult accounting and reporting problems. The foregoing discussion has attempted to highlight most of these problems as they relate to financial accounting. Because of the substantial amount of capital required and the relatively high degree of risk and uncertainty in the different phases of mining operations, it behoves management to recognize the demands of the investing public and attempt to be leaders rather than followers in their financial reporting practices.

7

TAXATION

Taxes play an important role in the financing and the day-to-day operations of mining companies. Familiarity with taxation concepts and the tax rules generally applicable to mining is useful in understanding this key area of finance within the industry. The objective of this chapter is first to provide an overview of the conceptual framework of tax systems and then to discuss some of the more commonly found aspects of taxation unique to the mining industry. It is hoped that the following discussion will assist mine management in gaining a better understanding of the impact of tax on financial planning.

Taxation is the aspect of mining economics which is often the most confusing to management who do not have a background in finance and accounting. This is understandable since:

1. Tax considerations, because they are governed by statute, will almost always require a high degree of professional advice
2. Tax is only visibly significant when a mine becomes profitable, and
3. Tax is not as controllable as most other costs without extensive planning

Because taxes, of all kinds, can be so substantial they are a factor requiring serious consideration at every stage of development of a mine – from initial exploration to exhaustion of the ore reserves. The individual prospector will be subject to personal tax on his income from his exploration activities; sales or transfer taxes may apply to purchases of equipment and other assets; property taxes may be assessed against land, buildings and equipment; and mining taxes or royalties may be levied on the output of a mine regardless of whether it is profitable; and finally, income taxes may take more than 50% of the profit from a mining venture. In short, tax may be a critical factor in the success or failure of a mining venture. It is essential that tax costs be minimized and this is only possible with proper planning.

No attempt will be made to provide details of any one particular tax system, except to illustrate a principle. There are too many tax systems within countries and states of the world to allow a detailed and comprehensive examination of all those which a mine manager might conceivably encounter. Even if space permitted an examination of specific tax systems, significant changes to tax laws are often made with such frequency that any detailed summary would quickly be obsolete. Also for these reasons, the responsibility for detailed planning and compliance should remain with in-house tax specialists and/or professional tax advisors.

Within the above constraints, the discussion of tax within this chapter, as outlined below, flows from the theoretical concepts to an overview of some of the more common peculiarities of tax laws as they pertain to mining companies:

1. Concepts of taxation
   (a) components
   (b) classifications
2. Taxation of mining income
   (a) domestic
   (b) international

It is hoped that this review of concepts and peculiarities will better enable mine management to deal confidently with tax specialists and advisors and to maximize the benefits of their advice.

CONCEPTS OF TAXATION

All governments must be able to purchase goods and services in order to maintain their existence and to fulfil their functions. The first and foremost source of revenue to fund these purchases is taxes.

Primitive forms of government usually confiscated specific goods and services directly. Modern, more sophisticated governments usually rely on taxing systems because of the perceived ability of such systems to meet some standard of equity in the spreading of the cost burden of government.

Components of tax systems

The basic components of most tax systems will include:

1. A definition of who or what is to pay the tax
2. The base on which the tax will be levied, and
3. A rate structure to be applied to the tax base

As an example, if income taxes are part of a country's tax system, they might be levied only on individuals or corporations who are considered residents of that country. As an alternative, income tax might be levied on all individuals who are citizens and all companies incorporated in a particular country, regardless of where they are resident and regardless of where the income is earned.

The base on which tax will be levied might be gross income with or without specific deductions. Alternatively, the starting point might be net income as computed in accordance with generally accepted accounting principles.

The rate of tax to be applied to the income might be a specific amount, a specific percentage or a percentage which changes according to the amount of taxable income.

The above components are common to most tax systems. Analyzing a particular tax system in terms of these components will allow rapid assimilation of the basic mechanics of the system and allow comparison with others.

Basic classifications

Taxes come in many forms. Looking at the above components from the viewpoint of attempting to establish a conceptual framework leads to broad methods of classifying and describing taxes.

Taxes can be classified in a theoretical manner according to the way they affect the taxpayer. That is, they can be classified as progressive or regressive, direct or indirect and neutral or non-neutral. Alternatively, they may be classified according to the base on which the tax is levied. The classifications here include income taxes, transfer or sales taxes, property taxes and head or per capita taxes.

Classification according to effect

Classifying a tax system according to its effect on the taxpayer is often useful in gaining an appreciation of the way a particular system operates.

Progressive or regresssive

A tax system can be classified as either progressive or regressive according to how heavily it falls on the taxpayer in relation to his ability to pay. Systems which tax the rich more heavily than the poor are generally said to be progressive. Most taxes on the income of individuals levied by Western nations are progressive in that the tax rate increases as higher levels of income are reached.

Taxes which are paid by both the rich and the poor equally without regard to ability to pay are termed regressive. Sales and transfer taxes tend to be regressive; thus basic necessities such as food are often exempted or only luxury items are taxed. If the sales tax applies to all transfers of goods and services, the tax paid as a percentage of income will tend to be higher for low income earners than for those with higher income.

Whether a tax system is progressive or regressive will seldom be apparent from the way in which corporations are taxed. Many systems allow for a lower rate of income tax on small organizations or low income earners but these advantages will seldom be significant to corporations involved in mining.

Direct or indirect

Another useful way of classifying taxes is according to whether they are actually borne by the person who pays them or whether they are simply passed on to someone else.

Direct taxes are those which are borne by those who pay them. Sales tax levied at the consumer level is a direct tax. Indirect taxes are those which can be passed on by the person paying the tax. Import taxes or sales tax levied at the manufacturer's level are examples of such a tax since the importer or manufacturer does not absorb the tax but simply adds it to his selling price. Although the tax is levied and paid by him it is ultimately borne by the consumer in the form of higher prices.

The distinction between a direct and indirect tax is seldom significant in analyzing the feasibility of a mining venture. It is irrelevant whether the tax is included in the acquisition costs of equipment, collected as a levy on real property, paid as a royalty or paid as an income tax on net profit. The essential point to be made is that a project must be capable of earning a net return on the owner's investment, after payment of all forms of taxes, before it can be considered viable.

Neutral or non-neutral

Taxes can also be classified according to the way they influence the taxpayer's decisions. A tax will be considered neutral if a taxpayer's decision would be the same regardless of whether the tax was applicable. Very few taxes or tax systems can be considered neutral.

Non-neutrality is not necessarily bad and can be an instrument of government political or economic policy. Investment incentives administered through the tax system may make the tax system non-neutral but at the same time they may also make a marginal mining proposition viable or allow an upgrading of mill and smelter equipment.

Classification according to tax base

Classifying a tax system according to its effect on the taxpayer is useful in describing and differentiating taxes conceptually. On the other hand, classifying taxes according to the base on which the tax is levied directly describes one aspect of the mechanics of the tax and is a more common way of classifying and identifying taxes.

Income taxes

Taxes based on income are not necessarily the major revenue earners in all countries, nor are they always the most visible. However, they are usually subject to more attention and critical analysis than any of the other forms of tax discussed below. Perhaps it is because they are usually more complex and therefore often subject to some degree of control or manipulation by the taxpayer. On the other hand, the concern may arise because the taxpayer views an income tax as a forced partnership with government on the profit which he has earned through his own efforts.

Income taxes are generally levied on individuals who are residents or citizens of a country or who are domiciled there. Corporations will usually be taxed on the basis of the jurisdiction of their incorporation. Most jurisdictions will tax both individuals and corporations who carry on business or otherwise receive income from activities carried on within their borders or on investments located there.

The more familiar form of income tax is a tax based on some concept of net profit. Income taxes based on net profit are more complex than simple royalties or other taxes applicable to gross revenue. Not only must revenue be determined but so must the allowable deductions. The profit which is taxable is usually determined in a way which is based on generally accepted accounting principles, but subject to adjustment to conform to specific rules which must be followed.

Taxes on gross revenue

Royalties are a form of tax which can be considered an income tax not based on a net profit concept. Royalties are usually calculated as a fixed amount per unit of production or as a percentage of gross revenue. Like the withholding taxes discussed above, royalties are usually payable regardless of whether a venture shows a net return after all expenses have been paid. For this reason royalties are often considered as a cost of production rather than a true income tax.

Another example of a tax based on gross revenue is the withholding tax, usually in the range of 5% to 40%, which is levied by most countries on interest and dividends paid to non-residents. The tax is usually required to be withheld by the person making payment to the non-resident. Although the rates of withholding tax are usually lower than most income taxes, no allowance is given for any expenses which might be applicable to the earning of the income.

Transfer or sales taxes

Transfer or sales taxes are levied on the transfer or sale of goods and services. The tax is usually based on a percentage of the sale price or the value at the time of transfer. To ensure that double tax does not result and that goods only bear tax once prior to reaching the end user, transfer taxes are usually levied at a particular level in the merchandising structure. For instance, tax may be payable only when goods reach the ultimate user or consumer. Alternatively, a tax may be levied at the last stage of manufacturing, before goods are sold to wholesalers.

An example of another way of solving the potential problem of double taxation is found in the Value Added Taxes (VAT) which are widely used by members of the European Economic Community. Although tax is collected on almost all transfers of property, where goods are subject to multiple transfers prior to reaching the end user, credit is given at each level for tax collected previously. The result is that each person in the manufacture–distribution chain pays a portion of the tax and the full tax on the price of the goods to the ultimate consumer is only paid once. To encourage exports, in most cases tax is not levied on goods sold out of the country.

Sales taxes have the advantage of being, in most cases, relatively simple to administer. They are therefore popular with political subdivisions of countries at the state or occasionally the municipal level.

Property taxes

Property taxes are a form of taxes which are popular with political subdivisions, particularly municipalities, primarily because of ease of administration. Property taxes are usually charged to the owners of the property at a percentage of some assessed value of the property. The assessed value may or may not be the same as the market value. Sometimes property taxes are based on a percentage of the real or theoretical rental which can be derived from the property.

Head taxes

A head tax or poll tax is the most simple form of tax. As the name implies it is levied on a per capita basis. In its most primitive form all inhabitants of a region would each be required to pay a specific amount. In a more modern context airport departure taxes which are levied as a specific amount on each passenger arriving at or departing from a particular airport can be considered to be head taxes.

Specific rules

The necessity for special or specific rules for the calculation of income subject to tax arises for several reasons:

1. To standardize profit measurement for taxation purposes
2. To allow government economic or political policy to be implemented through the income tax system
3. To minimize the cost of administering the tax system

The most important reason for specific rules is that generally accepted accounting principles are sufficiently flexible that strict reliance on them for calculation of profit might encourage manipulation to minimize or eliminate tax. Although full disclosure of accounting principles ensures that financial statements will be meaningful to users, revenue authorities will not accept full disclosure as a substitute for paying tax. Specific rules, even if they are arbitrary, are often necessary to eliminate alternatives and provide certainty of tax consequences.

Depreciation policy is an example of an area where most tax systems impose specific rules rather than relying on generally accepted accounting principles. Generally accepted accounting principles would normally sanction any method of amortization which allocates the cost of mine plant and equipment to the subsequent accounting periods in which the assets are used. However, what is reasonable is a matter of judgement regarding both the estimated useful life of an asset and the way in which its cost should best be allocated. This can result in a significantly wide range of acceptable depreciation policies.

For instance, if it is assumed that an ore body had a life of ten years it might be argued that the concentrator and other equipment should be depreciated straight-line and 10% of cost written off in each year. It might also be argued that since in later years the mill will require increasingly more costly maintenance, most of the initial cost should be depreciated in the first few years. The declining balance method of depreciation using a rate of, say, 20%, will accomplish this—depreciating 20% the first year, 20% of the remaining balance (i.e. 20% of 80% = 16%) in the second year and so on. This will result in over 65% of the cost of the asset being written off in the first five years. Using the same method, but increasing the rate to 30%, results in over 80% of the cost being written off in the first five years.

The range of acceptable alternatives illustrates the wide range of acceptable depreciation charges for accounting purposes. In order to reduce the opportunities for manipulating income by choosing a method which produces the best tax result, many tax systems prescribe specific rules for depreciating assets.

Other examples of specific rules to implement government policy are investment incentives and tax deductions for contributions to retirement plans. Common methods of providing incentives to acquire or upgrade plant and equipment are to offer accelerated depreciation or investment tax credits. Allowing employees a deduction in computing their income for amounts set aside in retirement plans is another example.

Reduced administrative cost of ensuring compliance with the tax rules explains the introduction of many specific rules to govern the types of income to be taxed and the type and amount of allowable deductions. If income is subject to tax on a gross basis and no deductions are allowed, the question of determining which expenses are necessary to the earning of that income is eliminated, thus reducing the costs of ensuring compliance. Costs may be further reduced by requiring that all employers deduct taxes from employees' wages and remit them to the government.

The above examples of reasons for specific rules for the calculation of taxable income are applicable to most types of income in most tax systems. However, the taxation of mining income probably involves the most complex and the greatest number of special rules. The balance of this chapter will be devoted to a discussion of these special rules and the reasons for their existence. The focus will be on those rules affecting corporations rather than other forms of organizations or individuals as this will be of primary interest to mine management.

TAXATION OF MINING INCOME

The major features of most income tax systems that are unique in their application to mining result from attempts to arrive at satisfactory and acceptable solutions to unique industry problems. Most of the problems arise from the nature of mining ventures as commercial enterprises and the need to satisfy conflicting objectives of government policy – stimulation of industry and the collection of tax.

The commercial features of mining ventures which are difficult to accommodate in a tax system are as follows:

1. Mining is a high-risk activity requiring a large capital investment which can seldom be fully financed with internally generated funds. The risk associated with mining ventures must be considered and the tax system must allow a return on investment sufficient to attract the required investment capital to the mining sector.
2. The time from initial exploration of a property to exhaustion of its ore reserves is invariably a period longer than the accounting period used to measure income for tax purposes. An attempt must be made to match costs and revenue over the life of a mine.
3. Mining is often carried on by large integrated companies on an international basis. Domestic tax rules governing individuals and entities incorporated and carrying on business in a country must therefore recognize and take into account the tax laws of other jurisdictions.

The above problems are magnified considering the constraints placed on tax systems, at least in most countries of the Western world. First, government revenue requirements must be met. Secondly, the tax system must serve to implement government policy. At the same time, it is expected that tax laws should be clearly understood and not subject to manipulation; that they must at least appear to treat individuals, small isolated ventures and large integrated mining companies equitably; and that they must do so at each and every stage of the development of a mine, from initial exploration to shutdown on exhaustion of the ore reserves.

These are difficult requirements to satisfy simultaneously. All that can often be hoped for is a satisfactory set of compromises. It is a matter of judgement as to what is satisfactory, and this in part explains why the taxation of mining income is often subject to frequent and radical change.

The major features of tax systems as they apply to mining will be discussed under the heading 'Domestic taxation'. This will refer to the taxation of operations within a particular country. The basic problems of 'International taxation' are discussed separately.

Domestic taxation

Mine management will seldom have direct responsibility for dealing with tax-related matters. However, an understanding of the basic features of the tax system governing the mine operation will allow better communication with accountants and professional tax advisors who must often rely on mine management for information necessary to solve tax-related problems.

The aspects of a country's domestic taxation policies which will be of prime concern to those in mine management can be segregated in four principal areas. These are the treatment of exploration and development expenses, depreciation and depletion policies, incentives and disincentives to mining which are incorporated in the tax system and the extent to which expenses can be transferred between taxpayers.

Exploration and development expenses
The treatment of exploration and development expenses is one of the most important items in the taxation of mining income. Exploration work is usually the first major expense in a sequence which may lead to an operating mine. In many instances, it is the only expense which will be incurred, since exploration of numerous properties may be undertaken without success.

The problem of accounting for exploration is attacked in most tax systems in one of two ways. Exploration may be considered essentially a sunk cost, the value of which is sufficiently uncertain that it cannot reasonably be capitalized and written off against the income of future accounting periods. It is therefore reasoned that exploration expense should be fully deductible for tax purposes in the year in which it is incurred. The United States and Canada, for instance, both allow exploration costs to be deducted in the year in which they are incurred, although in the United States the write-off must be recaptured if the property comes into commercial production.

Conversely, both successful and unsuccessful exploration may be considered part of the cost of finding properties, if any, which are viable. If this argument is accepted it follows that exploration expense should be capitalized. If exploration expenses are capitalized for tax purposes they are usually amortized on the basis of future production or at a specific percentage each year.

Brazil, for instance, requires exploration expense to be capitalized and amortized over the life of the mine on the units of production method.

If exploration is successful, massive expenditures will be required to develop a producing mine. The point at which exploration ceases and development begins is not always clear and can become a matter of contention in tax systems which distinguish between the two. Development is usually considered to have begun as soon as the existence of a commercially exploitable ore body has been established. By the time development is begun, the risk of not developing a viable producing mine is reduced considerably, even though it is not entirely eliminated. Development expenses are therefore usually required to be capitalized and amortized on the basis of future production or at a specific percentage each year.

Canada generally allows development expenses to be amortized at 30% each year on a declining balance basis. The United States allows development costs to be either written off or deferred and amortized on a basis related to the ore produced.

In most tax systems, the costs of acquiring mineral properties are usually treated in a manner similar to development costs in that they must be capitalized and written off against future income. However, unlike development costs, property acquisition costs are sometimes subject to depletion rules as discussed below. Very often, both acquisition costs and development costs will be immediately deductible if the property to which they relate is abandoned.

Depreciation and depletion

The amortization of the costs of fixed assets such as plant and equipment is an area where most tax systems find it necessary to resort to a set of more or less arbitrary rules to supplant those used for calculating depreciation for financial accounting purposes. In some tax systems, such as that of the United States, the range of acceptable alternatives is quite wide. However, most, such as Canada and Germany, require adherence to a straight-line or declining-balance method using fixed rates for specific classes of assets.

Depletion is a deduction in computing income which is meant to recognize, in some way, the utilization or wasting of a natural resource. Depletion is not allowed by all tax systems. Most income tax systems which do so will base the rate on a percentage of income or revenue or on the basis of production. The amount of depletion allowed in total may be unlimited or it may be based on an arbitrary fixed amount or some other factor such as total preproduction costs or property acquisition costs. If total depletion is not limited it can represent a deduction for tax purposes in excess of actual costs. This reduces both the apparent rate of income tax calculated as a percentage of book profit and the effective actual tax rate applicable to mining income.

In the United States, for example, depletion is allowed on either a cost or percentage basis, whichever is greater. Cost depletion is allowed based on production but is limited in total to the cost or other basis of the resource property. Percentage depletion is limited to the lesser of a percentage of gross income or 50% of taxable income from the property. The percentage of gross income used varies depending on the type of mineral.

In Canada, depletion equal to 25% of production profits is allowed. However, the cumulative total allowed is limited to 33⅓% of certain expenditures; generally these include Canadian exploration and development expenses and plant and equipment costs. This requirement to 'earn' depletion is considered effective in stimulating exploration and finding and developing new ore reserves within Canada.

Incentives
In order to encourage exploration activity and the development of new mines, most governments offer incentives of one kind or another and very often these are administered through the tax system. Although some incentives will be direct to the point that they may be considered to be government subsidies, indirect incentives may also be used to encourage specific types of activity.

Examples of more direct incentives encouraging mine development would be a tax holiday during which the income of a producing mine would be exempt from tax, and a favourable rate structure applicable to production income. Prior to 1971, Canada allowed a three year tax holiday for new mines. Ireland allowed a generous holiday of up to 20 years prior to 1974 when the qualifications for exemption were tightened and other incentives substituted.

Most countries do not technically apply a separate reduced tax rate to production income. However, the same effect can be achieved through the use of deductions for tax purposes over and above actual cash expenditures, such as depletion, as previously discussed.

Another way of offering an incentive is to accelerate the rate of deductibility of certain costs. Accelerated amortization of development expenses and depreciation of fixed assets are prominent examples of this type of incentive.

The length of the allowable amortization period for development expenses can significantly affect the cash flow from a successful venture. If development costs can be written off in full against production income, no tax will be payable until a mine has achieved a positive cumulative cash flow. On the other hand, if development expenses must be amortized for tax purposes over the expected life of the ore-body, it is likely that tax will be payable out of the first production revenue. This can have a significant and adverse effect on a project's return on investment.

Another incentive often administered through the tax system is a credit against income taxes payable based on a percentage of the acquisition cost of mining plant and equipment. Tax credits for investments in plant and equipment are usually in the 5 to 10% range. Both Canada and the United States offer Investment Tax Credits. In Canada, the credit reduces the base against which depreciation is claimed for tax purposes but in the United States it does not.

Indirect incentives offered through the tax system are often difficult to detect. For instance, if provisions exist to allow tax deductions for exploration work to be transferred between taxpayers, this will encourage individuals and small organizations having other taxable income to undertake exploration work. In the event that the exploration is not successful, it may be possible to recoup at least a portion of the expenses by effecting the transfer of their tax deductibility to another taxpayer.

In contrast, if deductibility of exploration expenses cannot be transferred, most exploration work will only be carried out by large integrated concerns who have other taxable income against which to offset the expense.

Transferability of expenses
In most instances, if production revenue is ever realized, it will be many years after the exploration and initial development work has been done. If, for tax purposes, expenses are deductible only in the year in which they are incurred, the possibility arises that production revenue might be fully taxable without any recognition being given to

expenses of prior years. Most tax systems recognize the inequity of such a result and provide for some means of effectively carrying forward the deductibility of certain expenses in the form of loss carryovers or by allowing deductions to be transferred to other taxpayers.

The United States allows net operating losses to be carried back three years and forward seven. In contrast, Chile allows only a two year carry forward and no carry back is permitted.

The rules for ensuring the availability of tax deductions for expenses incurred in prior years or by other taxpayers are usually complex and strictly interpreted. This is an important area in which it will usually be prudent to rely on professional advice.

Deferred taxes

The difference between book income and taxable income which arises from the use of different rates of amortizing costs for book purposes versus tax purposes is the basis for the concept of deferred taxes as a generally accepted accounting principle. When write-offs are accelerated for tax purposes the current tax payable expressed as a percentage of book income will appear disproportionately low. Because the ultimate quantum of the deduction remains the same and only the rate is different for book and tax purposes, any low apparent rates of current taxes payable resulting from accelerated tax write-offs will be offset by high apparent rates in the future when an unamortized balance will still be available as a deduction for book purposes but not for tax purposes.

In order to match tax costs against book income properly, the additional taxes which would be payable based on the difference between taxable and book income are calculated and shown as deferred income taxes. In later years when book income is lower than taxable income, this deferred tax is reversed so that the high actual current tax liability is offset and the charge against earnings is reduced. In this way it is hoped that a deduction and its tax effect are booked at the same time. The yearly tax charge against earnings will then remain fairly constant as a percentage of book income, barring changes in actual tax rates.

Unfortunately, the practicalities of commercial activity detract from the theoretical soundness of deferred taxes, at least within the time frames usually considered. Healthy organizations, especially in mining, are constantly embarking on new exploration programs and adding productive capacity. The result is that additional deductions are added continuously. If these deductions are subject to provisions for accelerated write-off for tax purposes, the deferred tax liability just continues to increase and never reaches the turn-around point where book deductions begin to exceed those available for tax purposes.

It is often argued that in this situation deferred taxes represent a contingent rather than reasonably certain liability and that therefore they should not be calculated and shown on the balance sheet. Only the liability for taxes currently payable would then be charged against book earnings. Alternatively it is argued that the deferred taxes should be shown but the amount should be discounted to take into account the time value of money. Neither of these methods of accounting for timing differences between book income and taxable income are generally accepted in the United States or Canada. In the United Kingdom, however, timing differences are taken into account only if they will be relevant in computing income in the foreseeable future, which is currently taken to be three years. Many believe the United Kingdom approach to deferred taxes to be far more practical than that of Canada or the United States.

International taxation

International taxation is more complex than domestic taxation simply because the tax systems of more than one country are involved. Fortunately mine management will seldom have occasion to consider international tax consequences without the involvement of tax specialists. However, an appreciation of certain basic principles will be useful, especially if a parent company or head office is not located in the same country as the operating mine. In this case some planning will almost certainly be necessary to ensure that overall tax is minimized. Implementation of such plans will be facilitated if management is aware of the considerations involved.

The problems of international taxation are not unique to the mining industry. Accounting for international business activities is conceptually difficult and conflicting theories may mean that there is more than one acceptable method of accounting in a given set of circumstances. In addition, political and economic policies will often be a primary factor in determining tax consequences.

Branch operations
Most countries impose tax on entities organized or incorporated under their jurisdiction on a global basis, that is, they include all income of the entity in the tax base regardless of where it is earned. When

activities are carried on as a branch operation in a foreign country the branch must first account to the foreign jurisdiction according to its tax laws. At the same time, the income and expenses of the branch will be included in computing income to be taxed in the home country according to its tax laws.

This dual reporting responsibility can lead to a number of problems – mainly in the determination of income to be taxed and the way in which taxes imposed by other jurisdictions are to be treated.

Some countries have been content to rely on generally accepted accounting principles in determining the income which they will tax. However, there are numerous types of income and expense which often cannot be clearly and definitely identified as being allocable to activities carried on in a particular jurisdiction. As a result, the possibilities of manipulating income to minimize the amount reported to higher tax rate jurisdictions are such that most countries have had to evolve sophisticated sets of rules to assist in determining how income and expense items are to be allocated between domestic and foreign sources.

Most countries allow a credit for foreign taxes paid in determining the tax payable under their own laws. All or a portion of the foreign taxes on foreign source income may be deductible in computing the tax payable to the home country. The extent of the deduction will usually be limited to the amount of tax which would otherwise have been payable had the income been from a domestic source.

Here again the problem of determining the amount of foreign source income is encountered. If a foreign jurisdiction has levies on certain income, but under domestic rules there is no income from that source, no foreign tax credit will be allowed for domestic tax purposes.

This type of problem will sometimes be mitigated by provisions allowing foreign taxes to be carried over and to be used as a credit in other years. If the difference between the income as calculated for domestic purposes is not permanent, the credit may then be taken in the year in which the income is recognized for domestic purposes.

Foreign taxes may also be allowed as a deduction in computing income subject to tax rather than as a credit against taxes payable. This result will be advantageous except where, for some reason, full credit for the foreign tax paid would not be allowed.

Foreign subsidiaries
Different problems arise when foreign operations are carried on in a foreign incorporated subsidiary rather than directly through a branch

operation of the parent company. Income earned by a foreign incorporated subsidiary will seldom be included in computing the income of the parent for tax purposes. Income and expenses of the subsidiary will be taxed by the foreign jurisdiction. Only when the income is distributed to the parent in the form of dividends will the laws of the home jurisdiction come into play. Most jurisdictions allow some sort of deduction from income or credit against taxes payable to ensure that income in the form of inter-corporate dividends is not subject to double taxation.

Carrying on operations through a foreign subsidiary can be advantageous in that the problem of ensuring that any foreign taxes paid can be utilized as a credit for domestic purposes may be eliminated. Further advantages will accrue if the tax rate in the foreign jurisdiction is less than the domestic tax rate. However, these advantages must be weighed against the disadvantage that any losses incurred in the subsidiary will not be deductible in computing the income of the parent for domestic tax purposes.

Normally, dividends paid by a foreign subsidiary to its parent will be subject to tax by the foreign country on a withholding basis when the dividends are remitted. The tax will vary from zero to a maximum of 40%. The tax will be applied to the gross dividends with no deduction for any expenses which may be applicable.

In addition to a withholding tax on dividends paid to non-residents, some countries also levy an equivalent tax on the earnings of a branch operation. In this case, the tax is usually levied at the time the income is earned rather than when it is repatriated. This is because earnings of a branch operation are subject to less control than the earnings of a subsidiary as they can usually be repatriated without formal declaration of a dividend.

Treaties

Almost all developed countries in the Western world have entered into a network of tax treaties to reduce the possibility of double taxation and tax evasion which can arise through international commercial activity. The tax treaties usually override the provisions of domestic law and are usually interpreted more liberally with a view to equity.

The mechanics for minimizing the incidence of double taxation are usually complete exemption of certain types of income from tax by one or both of the countries and reduced rates of withholding tax on items such as dividends, interest and royalties.

The treatment of treaty-governed income is often sufficiently worthwhile to structure commercial ventures to take advantage of beneficial treaty provisions. Sometimes the tax advantages can be optimized through the involvement of one or more other countries but this will require significant tax savings to justify the cost in terms of both the professional assistance required and the possible awkwardness of the resulting commercial structure.

Political and economic considerations

The dominance of political and economic considerations is a complicating factor in international taxation, particularly the taxation of mining income. Each country must find an acceptable balance between the need to control the utilization of its own natural resources and the need to attract investment capital. Clear-cut solutions to this problem are seldom found. Foreign ownership and control is often the price which must be paid for foreign investment, especially for developing nations. Attracting foreign investment may be necessary to ensure a healthy economy and a place in international commerce.

Attempts to balance these conflicting objectives usually result in the rules governing taxation of foreign organizations being different from those governing domestic entities. Similarly, but from another viewpoint, the rules governing the taxation of foreign source mining income will differ from those applicable to domestic source income. Usually both of these types of differences will affect the incentives included in the tax system—restricting them to domestic source income earned by domestic entities.

Most countries can be classified as either capital importing or capital exporting countries according to whether they need to attract foreign investment capital. Capital importing countries needing foreign investment to provide production capacity will tend to attract foreign capital by imposing low tax rates, thus allowing a higher return on investment. Investment and repatriation of foreign funds will not be restricted. Capital exporting countries and those whose desire for control of their own natural resources outweighs the need for foreign investment will often ensure that tax advantages, if any, are only available to domestically controlled entities. This may be an alternative to legislative restrictions such as requiring all foreign investment to take only a minority position in government or otherwise domestically controlled entities.

SUMMARY

An understanding of the tax environment in which decisions are made is essential to effective mine management. This chapter has attempted to survey most of the peculiarities in the taxation of mining income and to provide a framework for analysis and understanding. It is hoped that it will allow mine management to understand better the complexities of tax-related matters and to liaise efficiently with tax specialists and professional advisors.

8

CORPORATE SECURITY

Over the past several decades there has been a growing recognition by management of the benefits which may be derived from a properly planned and controlled system of corporate security. In the past, little attention was directed to this aspect of management since it was considered to be a non-productive function and often a necessary evil. With the rapid growth in complexity of today's mining organizations, international operations, and increased attentiveness of shareholders and major financial and lending institutions, management has come to recognize the necessity of various types of corporate security and of techniques they must utilize to monitor properly the corporate assets and create cost savings. The principal types of corporate security considered within this chapter include the internal audit, the external audit, audit committees and insurance and risk management. The amount of time and money directed to various aspects of corporate security will naturally depend on the size and complexity of the individual mining organization. The basic methods set out in this chapter can and should be applied as good management tools in any mining company.

INTERNAL AUDIT

Basic function and activity

The internal audit is a management control which measures and evaluates other controls. It is an independent appraisal activity within an organization for the review of accounting, financial and other operations as a service to management. The internal auditor's overall objective is to assist all members of management in their duties through objective comment, appraisal, analysis and recommendation of actions. There are as many ways to organize an internal audit as there are ways in which management is organized.

The basic concern of the internal auditor should be the value of his services to management. To attain his objectives he should examine:

1. The extent to which company assets are accounted for and protected from losses of all kinds
2. The extent of compliance with established policies, plans and procedures
3. The reliability of accounting and other data developed internally
3. The soundness, adequacy, and application of accounting, financial and operational controls
5. The quality of performance in the carrying out of assigned responsibilities

Operational audit concept

It should be emphasized that today's concept of internal auditing is one which extends beyond the traditional accounting and financial activities. Management should use the services of the internal auditor in virtually all the operating functions of mining activities under the term 'operational audit'. The auditor should specifically seek out aspects of operations in which waste, inefficiency and excessive costs could be reduced by the introduction of or improvements to existing management control systems.

Independence

Internal auditing can best be described as a staff function rather than a line function. The internal auditor should not exercise direct authority over any person in the organization whose work he reviews. Independence is essential. The status of the internal auditor and the support accorded him by management will determine the value and range of services which management will get from him. To ensure maximum independence the senior internal auditor should report to the senior financial officer of the company, to the chief operating officer, or even to the audit committee of the Board of Directors.

Reporting responsibilities

Because the internal auditor should not exercise any direct authority over the persons whose work he reviews, his written report should be delivered to his immediate superior who will in turn transmit it to the individual responsible for the function that has been reviewed. Effective preliminary communication within the review is essential to eliminate misunderstandings, errors, unworkable recommendations and internal dissention. Considerable benefit may be derived from informal preliminary review with department personnel. Including the personnel concerned in such discussions promotes a team spirit and often brings to light shortcomings which may not otherwise be detected. Employees will also derive considerable personal satisfaction from being included in the contribution to more effective and efficient management controls.

Relationship with external audit

The principal differences between internal and external audit are best summarized as follows: -

1. Internal audit is performed by an employee of the company whose primary concern is in serving the needs of management
2. External audit is performed by a professional public accountant who is engaged independently to report to third parties, usually the shareholders, on the financial statements or other financial data

When internal auditing is superimposed on all other forms of management controls, the resultant accounting figures should be accurate and reliable. Under these circumstances the external auditor can establish a sound basis for the expression of his opinion on the company's financial statements with an independent examination which involves only a minimum amount of verification. This can be done only after the external auditor has carefully reviewed the scope and thoroughness of the internal auditor's program and determines the reliability of that program. Such a review will also include measuring the general competence of the internal audit staff, their position and reporting responsibilities within the company and particularly their independence and freedom from operating responsibilities.

To achieve the maximum external audit cost savings, the internal audit function, as it relates to financial reporting, should be completely co-ordinated with the external audit. Internal control reviews, systems flow charting, procedural test programs and many other audit functions should be prepared and carried out by the internal auditor only after full discussion with the external auditors. The audit files and reports should be made available to the external auditor together with complete details of the ultimate disposition of all major recommendations on internal control, accounting and reporting practices.

Internal audit procedures and reports

Once the basic principles of management control are established through the use of an internal audit department it is appropriate to cite some areas of major concern in a mining organization where such services have proven to be of substantial value through long and short-term cost savings:

1. Camp accommodation – by implementing effective controls and verification procedures on 'charge outs' and costs
2. Sales taxes – by proper review and instructions on procedures for exemptions and recoveries using independent sales tax experts where appropriate
3. Government grants – by familiarization of appropriate departments with grants and special loans available such as for roads, personnel and training
4. Freight – by monitoring terms of major freight contracts, particularly escalation clauses based on carrier cost increases
5. Purchasing – by ensuring proper controls and procedures relating to competitive bidding and quotations, volume purchasing, purchase discounts and payment discounts
6. Short-term investments – by review of budget and cash flows to ensure the maximum available return is obtained from short or long-term cash surplus
7. Stores and materials handling – by review of physical safeguards, receipt and delivery procedures, perpetual inventory systems and returns to suppliers to satisfy efficient physical movement requirements without prejudicing accounting and physical controls
8. Insurance – by review of insurance coverages in relation to management's stated policies to satisfy adequacy of coverage including utilization of independent experts for review of terms and rates
9. Plant and facilities construction – by review of cost plus contracts, setting up and monitoring controls on labour and service charges, overhead and camp costs, purchasing and approval systems, and cash requirements and utilization

EXTERNAL AUDIT

Basic function and purpose

In order to understand properly the use of the external audit as a management control one must first understand the relationship of the external auditor to the company, its management and its shareholders.

It is a popular misconception that the financial statements are prepared by the external auditor and thus are his representations. This is not so. The financial statements are representations of management and are the means by which management reports the financial results of its stewardship to the shareholders and other third parties. In the purest sense the external auditor's responsibility for the statements he has examined is confined to the expression of his opinion on them. If, after his audit examination, the external auditor agrees as to the fairness of the representations in the financial statements he will issue a 'clean opinion'; if he does not agree and discussions with management do not result in changes in disclosure, then the external auditor will qualify his opinion, give an adverse opinion, or simply deny an opinion. The external auditor will naturally discuss matters of material consequence with management, but it should be emphasized that the financial statements are those of management. The external auditor cannot insist on the nature of financial disclosure in the statements other than to disclose full details as part of his opinion in his report. For instance, if management has decided to amortize preproduction costs of a new open pit mine over a period of twenty years and the total ore reserves indicate a life of only eight years, the external auditor has no right to change the financial statements to reflect more fairly the financial position and results of operations. Naturally his first course of action will be to try to convince management that their treatment of preproduction amortization is wrong and that the proper amortization period is eight years. If management is not willing to follow such recommendations, then the auditor will qualify his opinion, setting out his reasons and his opinion as to the dollar amounts involved.

Independence

The independent audit which provides the added credibility to management's annual financial representations to shareholders is called for by law in most countries. In the case of special purpose statements an audit is usually demanded by the third parties for whose use the statements are intended. It is only natural then that those who rely on the external audit opinion be concerned regarding the qualifications of the auditor. Chartered Accountants (Canada, United Kingdom, Australia) and Certified Public Accountants (United States) form the largest professional public accounting and auditing bodies. They are recognized for their technical competence because of rigid prequalifying training, examinations and period of internship in a public accounting office.

While their technical abilities are important, the greatest strength and asset that the external auditors have is their independence. In most areas of the world, legislation governs their independence by prohibiting an external auditor from being an employee, officer, director or shareholder of the company for which he acts as auditor. For those few who are unscrupulous, legislation presents no particular obstacle; therefore true independence may better be described as a state of mind resulting in the ability to think and act in an independent and professional manner. Unless the external auditor is independent, his opinion is of no more value to a shareholder or other third party than the representations of management.

Reporting responsibilities

The most common form of auditors' report is the one to the shareholders found in the company's published annual report. To provide a better understanding of the auditors' report, one should examine the normal two paragraphs of the report. The first paragraph is usually described as the 'scope' paragraph where the auditor identifies the company, the date of the financial statements, the period of the earnings and other statements, and outlines the scope of his examination. The second paragraph is known as the 'opinion' paragraph in which the auditor gives his opinion of the fairness of the financial statements, their conformity with generally accepted accounting principles and the application of the principles on a basis consistent with the preceding reporting period. The wording of audit reports is governed by legislation in many areas of the world; however, all convey the same basic message.

The standard audit report which is acceptable in most of Canada, the United States and the United Kingdom is as follows:

Auditors' report to the shareholders

We have examined the balance sheet of the XYZ Mining Corporation Ltd as of December 31, 19-2 and the related statements of earnings, retained earnings and changes in financial position for the year then ended. Our examination was made in accordance with generally accepted auditing standards and accordingly included such tests of accounting records and such other auditing procedures as we considered necessary in the circumstances. We previously made a similar examination for the year ended December 31, 19-1.

In our opinion, the accompanying financial statements present fairly the financial position of the company as of December 31, 19-1 and 19-2 and the results of its operations and the source and use of its working capital for the years then ended in conformity with generally accepted accounting principles applied on a consistent basis.

Chartered Accountants

Date
City

Qualified audit reports

A qualified audit report will contain a middle paragraph setting out the details of the qualification and the opinion paragraph will be modified accordingly. Reasons for qualifications and other variations to audit reports vary directly in relation to those insoluble differences which occasionally arise between the external auditor and management. Because his report is rendered in an independent capacity the external auditor must retain final authority in the wording of it. A brief outline of some of the reasons for qualification of audit reports is as follows:

1. Limitations in the scope of examination as requested by management. Other reasons, such as not attending a supplies inventory count at a remote location, may not result in a qualification if the amounts are not material; however, the same circumstances as applied to a material portion of concentrate or supplies inventory would give rise to a qualification and possibly even a denial of opinion by the auditor if other acceptable methods of verification of the quantities and dollar values are not available. An example of a qualification of this nature would be:

   We were unable to satisfy ourselves regarding the existence of supplies inventory valued at $500 000 at one of the project camps which was inaccessible to us.
   In our opinion, except for the effect of adjustments, if any, which may have been determined to be necessary had we been able to observe the supplies as explained in the preceding paragraph, these financial statements present fairly. . .

2. Deviation from generally accepted accounting principles, such as failure to provide for depreciation of fixed assets or amortization of preproduction costs will almost certainly give rise to a qualification along the lines of:

   No provision has been made for depreciation of fixed assets during the year. Had provision been made on a basis consistent with the preceding year, net income for the year and retained earnings at the end of the year would have been reduced by $400 000; income taxes payable would have been reduced by $400 000 and working capital would have been increased by $400 000.

In our opinion, except that the company did not record depreciation for the year as referred to in the preceding paragraph, these financial statements present fairly. . .

3. Failure to disclose significant information
4. Disagreement on valuation
5. Inconsistencies in the application of generally accepted accounting principles
6. Failure to adhere to tax-allocation accounting

As previously pointed out, the financial statements are the representations of management. If management does not agree with the external auditor the financial statements need not be changed. However, management must realize that it is then the duty and responsibility of the external auditor to express his disagreement in his audit report. It should be pointed out that in some jurisdictions regulatory bodies such as securities commissions frown on and even refuse to accept financial statements where the audit report is qualified because of certain types of management decision which give rise to the qualification.

Fraud and errors

The external auditor's examination, which forms the basis for the expression of his opinion, is based on a review of systems and controls with such tests as he deems appropriate to satisfy himself of their adequacy. Other verification procedures are employed to validate cash, investments, concentrate settlements, concentrate and stores inventories, plant and equipment, preproduction and deferred costs, trade payables, long-term debt and capital stock. It must be emphasized that modern audit techniques are not 'specifically' designed to detect fraud or errors. None the less the modern audit should bring to light any fraud or errors which would have a material effect on the financial position or operating results of a company.

Special purpose reports

From the point of view of the corporate officers, the annual shareholders' audit is of limited internal value since its primary purpose is to satisfy the legal obligations of the company. Most external auditors go beyond the statutory report and provide the management team with a post audit or management letter which gives observations and recommendations about system and control weaknesses and breakdowns as well as other comments which the auditor believes would be of assistance to management in their control of operations. Some governments require that such a letter be provided.

Other special services offered by external auditors include:

1. Audits of financial statements for use in prospectuses and for filing with securities commissions on such occasions when the company wishes to be listed, sell capital stock, or issue long-term debt to the public
2. Review of interim financial statements or financial information which is to be provided to shareholders and/or securities commissions
3. Assistance in preparation of cash flow studies and income projections for use with feasibility studies
4. Special purchase audits of companies or assets being acquired through purchase and/or merger
5. Advice on matters of taxation including income taxes, special mining taxes, sales taxes, property and inventory taxes
6. Special fraud investigations where suspicion has been aroused and independent professional advice is deemed necessary
7. Special services relative to design and implementation of employee remuneration and bonus plans
8. Special reports to third parties on determination of joint-venture profits, royalty or other carried interests in their mineral properties
9. Systems and controls design and modification to suit operational changes and to provide management with more current or meaningful financial or statistical data
10. Modification and improvement of systems of internal control including those related to computer-based systems
11. Special investigations under insurance claims, particularly use and occupancy/loss of income claims

External audit procedures

Having accepted the appointment, most auditors will confirm this in writing describing the specific terms of their engagement. Special service engagements should also be confirmed in writing in order to avoid any misunderstanding.

Because the external auditor will not verify, add or otherwise check every transaction during the period, it is important that management understand the basic techniques used by external auditors in the course of their examination. The basic approach, as outlined earlier, in the most ideal circumstances is carried out by or in conjunction with the internal auditors. More often than not, however, this is not possible or practical, and the external auditor must perform the work himself.

In the broadest sense the approach includes functional tests and period-end validation. The functional tests are based on and include an understanding of the operations of the company, the charting of the systems, evaluation of internal controls, tests of the system and internal controls, and evaluation of the results of the tests. All these tests form part of the basis for his opinion. The period-end validation procedures include physical examination or independent confirmation of assets and liabilities at the date of the financial statements. Valuation methods used by management for determining concentrate and supply inventories, depreciation of mine and mill equipment, and amortization of preproduction and depletion of mineral properties will all come under their external auditor's scrutiny. In many instances the external auditor will have to rely on opinions of other independent parties, particularly for weight surveys of concentrate and crushed ore stockpiles, title opinions on mineral properties, and geologists' opinions for ore reserves. It becomes obvious that the external audit is not performed as an exact science nor will all figures necessarily be correct to the dollar. Materiality is the keyword and unless a multitude of smaller items compound to a material adjustment, the external auditor will bring the items to the attention of management but not suggest changes to the financial statements.

The popularity of December 31 as a fiscal year end has resulted in modifications to period-end verification procedures. The problems involved in completing audits of a major number of corporations all at the same time has forced the external auditor to adopt pre-year-end cut-off points for asset and liability validation. A December 31 year-end may be audited relying on validation procedures carried out as far ahead as October 31 with appropriate but limited update procedures being performed immediately after the year-end to allow expression of an opinion as at December 31. This modified approach may be used only in circumstances where good internal controls exist and seasonal fluctuations can be predicted with a high degree of accuracy.

AUDIT COMMITTEES

Evolution

The audit committee evolved at a time when other committees of the Board of Directors were becoming a very large element in the operations of business at the board level. Two basic factors were primarily responsible for this change. First, the corporations for which the Boards of Directors are legally accountable have become so large and complex in many cases that a specialization of tasks at the board level becomes necessary, as specialization has become necessary in overall corporate management. Secondly, as a result of new legislation and court actions instigated by shareholders and others which impose on directors stringent rules of conduct and liability, it has become necessary for a director of a company to become much more familiar with the state of affairs existing in that corporation. The general approach to audit committees is the same in all corporations having one. There are no peculiarities in the mining industry which would affect an audit committee.

Committee structure

The potential benefits of audit committees depend largely on careful planning and organization of their activities. This planning begins with the selection of committee members.

It is best that audit committees be kept fairly small so that they may meet easily and function efficiently. Generally there must be at least three members, but a committee of more than six is likely to be unwieldy. In the early days of audit committees the Board of Directors *en bloc* was often appointed. These committees on the whole were too large to act efficiently.

Audit committees must have a majority of non-executive or outside directors to preserve the independence of the overall audit. Ideally the members should have a practical and theoretical knowledge of business and finance to assist them in their review of the financial statements and all other matters with which the audit committee becomes concerned. In the United States the outside directors on the audit committee cannot be related to senior corporate officers.

It is a moot point whether senior management should be members of or should attend the meetings of the audit committee, and some companies have constituted their audit committees so that they do not include any insiders. Because company officers are usually the best sources of information needed to evaluate financial statements, it may be necessary for the chief financial officer to attend the meetings.

While its success depends to a large degree on the competence of its members, acceptance by senior management of the role of the audit committee is very important as well. The ideal audit committee would consist of one insider and two or more outsiders with financial reporting and accounting experience and with some direct experience of the business in which the company is involved.

Legislation usually does not stipulate the length of service for the audit committee members, but it would be ideal, if sometimes difficult, to rotate the membership on a three year basis. This goal is best achieved on a committee of several members with staggered terms of office so that continuity is maintained.

A typical audit committee will be structured and have basic responsibilities more or less as follows:

1. Corporations offering securities to the public shall have an audit committee of not fewer than three directors to be elected by the Board of Directors
2. The majority of the committee cannot be officers or employees of the corporation or its affiliates
3. The committee is to review the annual financial statements before approval by the board
4. The company's auditor is entitled to receive notice of all meetings and has the right to appear before and be heard by the committee at any meetings
5. Any audit committee member may require attendance by the auditor at every audit committee meeting
6. The auditor and any member of the committee may call a meeting of the committee
7. The directors shall forthwith notify the audit committee and the auditor of any error or misstatement of which they become aware in a financial statement on which the auditor or a former auditor has reported

Legislation varies by jurisdiction, but the thrust is essentially the same.

Committee duties and responsibilities

The various laws establishing audit committees say little about what the audit committee should do. To fill this gap, most of the larger public accounting firms issue their own guidelines and ideas on the duties and responsibilities of audit committees.

Within the general framework of the statutory responsibility of the audit committee, the following main purposes of audit committees have been identified. In order of importance, they might be ranked as follows:

1. To relieve the Board of Directors of details regarding the review of the results of the independent audit
2. To serve as an independent review function of the company's operations and its annual financial statements before their submission to the Board of Directors for approval
3. To provide non-officer directors with direct and more personal contact with independent auditors
4. To give additional attention to the audit function performed by the independent auditors
5. To relieve the Board of Directors of details regarding the review of the annual financial statements
6. To give attention to the internal control functions of a company
7. To relieve the Board of Directors of details regarding the arrangements for the independent audit and the nomination of the independent auditors
8. To assist the Board of Directors in their selection of independent and external auditors

All these purposes relate more or less directly to the annual financial statements and the audit opinions given on them. Increasingly audit committees, either through their own initiative or because the Board of Directors has specifically widened the terms of reference, concern themselves with many more diverse matters such as the existence and quality of the company's system of internal control; the quality and depth of staffing in the company's accounting and financial departments; the impact on the company's financial statements of proposed changes in generally accepted accounting principles; the quality of the company's internal audit program or, if none exists, the desirability of establishing such a program; the company's accounting principles generally with particular regard perhaps to income recognition, capitalization, and depreciation policy; transactions involving questionable or illegal payments; and other potentially contentious areas.

Credibility and objectivity

The board is responsible for providing the shareholders and the investing public with full and complete financial reports. It should welcome the appointment of an audit committee and should do its best to ensure that the committee members are well qualified to pass judgement on behalf of the board on the matters laid before them. They have a fiduciary relationship to ensure, on behalf of the shareholders, that the company is managed in the best possible manner. Part of that stewardship involves the accurate accounting for the operations of the corporation and proper presentation of financial information to shareholders. The audit committee is in a better position to fulfil this function than the board as a whole. This committee should provide additional protection for directors. An effective audit committee cannot help but enhance the credibility and objectivity of corporate financial reporting.

There is certainly no doubt that one of the most significant corporate developments in recent years has been the emergence of the audit committee. It has brought into sharper focus two important issues in the business world today: public confidence in financial reporting, and the responsibility and accountability of directors.

INSURANCE AND RISK MANAGEMENT

Risk management

Risk management is a business and management tool designed to minimize as much as possible pure risk losses. The task is usually performed by a company employee, the risk manager in a large corporation or the senior financial officer in a smaller one, working with a professional insurance broker. The risk management system breaks down into five major areas as discussed in the following paragraphs.

Identification of risk

Management must determine what hazards create the risks of accidental loss. This can be done by the broker or risk manager using a Risk Analysis or Survey form. This is an important and time-consuming task, as a great deal of information about operations, plans, assets, and products will be needed. Management should be prepared to provide full information including financial statements. This work may often be performed gratuitously in anticipation of the broker securing your account, but beware of a superficial job. It may be worth paying a fee or making some commitment to ensure a detailed survey and full report. Once the risks have been determined it is necessary to classify them into those which could have a significant effect on corporate results and those which would have an insignificant effect.

Elimination and/or control

Determine if significant risks can be avoided or eliminated. Risks can be avoided by not engaging in hazardous operations and can often be eliminated by passing the responsibility to a supplier, customer or independent contractor. Responsibility for loss in transit can be eliminated by selling FOB (free on board) your mill.

Control or remove risks that cannot be escaped. This is one of the most important fields in risk management. It calls for the fullest co-operation between management, engineering and design personnel on the one side and brokerage and underwriting personnel on the other side.

Examples of controlling risks are:

1. Employee safety programs
2. Selection and proper installation of safe machinery
3. Sprinkler systems with adequate water supply
4. Fire divisions between large mill areas
5. Good maintenance and housekeeping
6. Adequate fire fighting equipment and trained personnel

Insurance program

Meeting significant losses that cannot be reduced or eliminated will be accomplished by the establishment of a sound insurance program. Larger corporations may wish to consider self insurance and the use of captive insurers in order to retain some portion of premium funds within the overall corporate group. The insurance program including types of coverage are dealt with in greater depth later in this chapter under the heading 'Insurance program guide'.

Insurance broker

An insurance broker should be carefully selected. Price should not be the only determinant. The corporate insurance manager should ask to meet the people who will actually service the account and determine their qualifications. A good broker need not be large but he must have know-how and experience in handling similar accounts. The broker should have a general knowledge of plant and mill engineering and the ability to prepare plans, diagrams and reports to underwriters.

Most brokers will assign an account executive and one or more back-up personnel to handle your account. These people should determine your general attitude or insurance philosophy and then should complete a detailed Risk Analysis form to determine those risks which could cause a serious loss. The Risk Analysis form should be co-ordinated with an inspection of your premises and should be followed by a full report covering such things as loss prevention, risk control and recommended insurance and self-insurance.

When the report is submitted and a decision on the type of coverage made, the broker's 'placing' or 'marketing' department will go to work and place portions of your risk with one or several insurance companies or underwriters. Your broker should at all times endeavour to secure the coverages required at the lowest possible cost from sound, reputable insurers. The insurance that is arranged will initially be evidenced by 'binders' or 'cover notes' and these will later be replaced by policies or insurance contracts. It is imperative that the mining company insurance manager read all insurance policies. No matter how knowledgeable the broker, he may overlook an important point that will be noticed and brought to his attention when the policies are carefully reviewed.

As an insured, you have certain obligations to your underwriters and broker and these include:

1. Prompt advice in the matter of changes
2. Prompt submission of reports
3. Payment of premiums as agreed
4. Prompt delivery of loss claims with full details

One important aspect of any insurance program is the regular review. Your broker should – at least annually and sometimes as often as monthly – meet with your staff to ensure that all changes affecting insurance and risk management are properly communicated and acted on.

Underwriters and insurance companies

Insurance underwriters, insurers or insurance companies are one of the two major parties involved in every contract of insurance. Insurers provide the financial security of ability to pay insured losses should they occur. The insurer may be a stock company, a mutual company, a Lloyd's association or in special cases some other type of organization. Clients primarily rely on their broker to select sound and capable insurers. The broker should consider the following factors:

1. Licensing: the insurer must be licensed to transact business at the location of your property.
2. Financial: most licensed insurers are carefully scrutinized each year by special insurance departments of government and do not receive

their annual licence renewal unless they have met prescribed standards. You may wish to check further by using one of the published guides that rate insurance companies according to their financial standing, policyholder service and in various other ways.

3. Claims: in general, companies provide similar claims service. Some, however, tend to follow insurance contracts exactly while others may be more liberal in their interpretation, often applying a more up-to-date wording or their own interpretation of policy conditions if this is of benefit to the insured.

4. Engineering: some companies provide valuable inspection and engineering services and these can be used to advantage as part of the overall risk management program.

Insurance program guide

Table 8.1 is intended to serve as a guide to the types of insurance that could be applicable to a mining operation. There are many additional types of insurance that have only limited application to the mining industry and hence have not been included. In addition, details of all the various endorsements and extensions that can be provided in connection with specific types of policy are not included here. Insurance policies break down into a few basic categories, those insuring physical property, those insuring indirect losses arising out of physical property, those insuring liability risks, surety bonds, combination policies, those insuring loss of earnings and other miscellaneous policies. Policies insuring physical assets and indirect losses arising from physical assets can generally be broken down into those which insure specified perils, such as fire and windstorm and those which cover all risks except, of course, those risks that are excluded. In reviewing a named-perils type of policy it is essential to study both the perils covered and the exclusions. In reviewing an all-risk policy, special attention should be paid to the exclusions. In reviewing these policies it should not be assumed that all-risk forms are always broader than named-perils forms. Some named-perils policies insure risks that are specifically excluded under all-risk forms. Most liability insurance policies provide protection if the insured is legally liable for damages because of bodily injury or property damage. Some forms include libel and slander and some include errors and omissions or professional liability.

Most mining companies would be well advised to pay particular attention to indirect and consequential losses. Use and occupancy or business interruption policies insure the loss of earnings and require

TABLE 8.1

	Type of insurance	Exploration	Plant construction	Mining and milling operations	Layup
1.	General liability insurance	*	*	*	*
2.	Non-owned auto insurance	*	*	*	*
3.	Fire or all-risk insurance (on buildings, equipment, supplies and other physical assets)	*	*	*	*
4.	Insurance on inventory (particularly concentrate in transit)			*	
5.	All-risk office equipment insurance	*		*	*
6.	Tenant's liability insurance (rented offices and other premises)	*	*	*	*
7.	Business interruption insurance		*	*	
8.	Extra expense insurance		*	*	
9.	Employee dishonesty (fidelity) insurance	*	*	*	*
10.	Auto insurance	*	*	*	*
11.	Life, pension and group insurance (for employees and executives)	*	*	*	*
12.	Workmen's compensation	*	*	*	*
13.	Medicare	*	*	*	
14.	Marine insurance (work-boat, barges and cargo shipments)	*	*	*	*

No.	Coverage				
15.	Performance bonds (guaranteeing performance of construction contracts and labour and material bonds from contractors)		*		
16.	'Wrap Up' programs providing liability and course of construction coverage to owner and all contractors and sub-contractors				
17.	Boiler and machinery insurance		*	*	
18.	Aircraft insurance (owned, non-owned and airstrip)	*	*	*	*
19.	Coverage on employees' personal effects (bunkhouses)		*	*	
20.	Directors' and Officers' liability	*	*	*	*
21.	Credit insurance		*	*	
22.	Transportation insurance				
23.	Professional liability (of employed architects, engineers and medical personnel)	*	*	*	
24.	Bullion floater				

particular attention. For example, an isolated mining operation could be shut down and lose its entire income for several months owing to the destruction of a related townsite housing its employees. A mill could be shut down because of the breakdown of a major piece of equipment or because of the interruption of power supply owing to damage at a power plant. Indirect or consequential loss could also arise owing to the destruction of transportation facilities such as docks or the transport ships themselves.

Particular attention should be given to the special risks that arise during construction. The failure of a major contractor involved in mill townsite or tunnel construction could cause great hardship to the developing organization and extremely bad community public relations can be incurred if a major contractor or sub-contractor fails to meet accounts payable to local suppliers. Both of these risks can be protected by requesting performance and labour and material payment bonds from contractors engaged on a project. Construction work is frequently carried out before fire prevention services are installed or before the surrounding areas are cleared or protected by fire access roads. A new plant is particularly vulnerable at this stage and the owner should ensure that the broadest type of insurance protection is provided.

Table 8.1 should serve as a basic guideline to management and, in particular, to the individual charged with the responsibility for risk management and related coverage.

CONCLUSION

The foregoing chapters have covered a broad range of subjects from the finding, development and construction to the operation of a mine. In each case an attempt has been made to relate the geological or engineering function to the finance related function.

Virtually every mine is owned, in some way or other, by the public. Management is becoming increasingly aware of their responsibility to public ownership to produce the best possible results within their organization. These results can only originate from the finding of a mine but the results are communicated by means of financial reporting, in a nutshell, the bottom line. Is the company making a satisfactory profit? In the end all efforts are directed to the achievement of the best possible return on investment. It is for this reason that the 'compleat' mine manager must always be aware of the ultimate financial effect of operational decisions.

In times of rapid technological change old ways are discarded for the new. Mini-computers, advanced communication techniques, improved transportation concepts, to name only a few, require a constant updating of knowledge. Modern management cannot be expected to be all things to all men. As a result many of the tasks once performed entirely by management are being done with the assistance of independent specialists. These are the tools that management must use to achieve the desired result. Just as operational techniques change so do financial concepts. Corporate and securities laws, tax laws, accounting reporting requirements, all have changed over the years, some with an incredible frequency. Once again, specialists are available to assist management. Even in an age of rapid change management must have a basic knowledge of corporate finance. While many of the 'bells and whistles' have undergone radical change over the years, most of the basic principles of financial management set out in the preceding chapters have stood the test of time.

I hope that what I have written will serve as a stimulant to those involved in mine management, or aspiring to be, and provide them with a better understanding of some of the corporate and financial considerations that lead to better management.

APPENDIX

Sample general ledger code of accounts for use during preproduction and construction

---

Petty cash
Bank account
Short-term investments
Prepaid insurance
Deferred expenses
Accounts receivable
*Plant, buildings and equipment
Land
*Mineral claims
*Shaft sinking and lateral development
*Pilot plant operation
*Plant operations
*General and administrative expenses
*Surface exploration and diamond drilling
*Technical and economic statistics
*Feasibility study
Pit mining costs
Pre-incorporation expenses
Cost of incorporation
Accounts payable
Accruals
Holdbacks payable
Wages payable
Accrued workmen's compensation
Accrued holiday pay
Interest earned
Share capital issued
Discount on shares issued
Subscribers

---

*Indicates that there is a subsidiary ledger code of accounts (attached).

Sample subsidiary ledger code of accounts during preproduction and construction

---

PLANT, BUILDINGS AND EQUIPMENT

Main sub-accounts

Site services
Service building
Headframe, shafthouse and ore bins
Hoist house
Crushing, screening and sampling
Mill
Power supply
Tailings
Mobile equipment
Underground equipment
Office equipment
Water supply
Camp
Engineering and construction management
Townsite

Sub-sub-accounts
Site services
Clearing and grubbing
Roads and yards
Water lines
Compressors and distribution
Sewage
Fire protection
Oil tank farm
Yard lighting
Telephone

Service building
Site excavation and backfill
Concrete
Structure
Powder magazine and cap shed

Plumbing and heating
Furniture
Equipment
Electrical

Headframe, shafthouse and ore bins
Excavation and backfill
Building foundations
Collar
Shafthouse cladding
Headframe
Ore bin
Equipment
Heating, piping and drains
Mine air heating
Electrics

Hoist house
Excavation and backfill
Building foundations
Hoist foundations
Structure
Hoisting ropes
Hoisting equipment
Compressors
Plumbing and heating
Electrical building and power

Crushing, screening and sampling
Site
Concrete footings (including bins)
Structure
Equipment
Sampling plant
Miscellaneous equipment
Electrics

Mill
Site
Concrete foundations – building
Concrete foundations – equipment

Structure
Conveyor hopper enclosure
Laboratory building
Laboratory equipment
New lab building
Equipment
Plumbing and heating
Furniture
Thickener
Electrics
Controls

Tailings
Clearing
Road
Dam
Pipe
Pumps
Reclaim

Water supply
Roads and clearing
Housing
Tank housing
Pumps
Pipes
Water supply wells
Storage tank
Propane heaters and furnace
Electrics

Camp
Site
Bunkhouses
Cookery
Office
Shops and service building
Recreation building
Water supply
Services
Office equipment

Geology and engineering
Miscellaneous

Engineering and construction management
Internal engineering
Outside engineering
Field supervision
Travelling and miscellaneous

Townsite
Land
Clearing
Water
Power
Roads
Housing
Apartments
Fire prevention
Recreation
Other public facilities

MINERAL CLAIMS (AND OPTIONS)

Main sub-accounts

Diamond drilling
Percussion drilling
Geology and mapping
Land surveyors
Trenching
Assaying
Core splitting and logging
Overhead
Line cutting
Claims
Claims staked re-proposed future use

SHAFT SINKING AND LATERAL DEVELOPMENT

Main sub-accounts

Shaft sinking
Stations

Loading pockets
Mine sumps
Lateral development
Underground diamond drilling

Sub-sub-accounts (for each main sub-account, where appropriate)

Contract
Power and signal lines
Ground support (rock, bolts, timber)
Air, ventilation and water lines
Track and installation
Supplies
Shaft changeover

PILOT PLANT OPERATIONS

Main sub-accounts

Crushing and sampling
Grinding and flotation
Mill equipment rentals
Chemical laboratory
Mill supervision
Labour
Supplies
Contractor

PLANT OPERATIONS

Main sub-accounts

Hydro
Heating
Utilities, water and sewer operation and maintenance
Shops
Vehicles
Cookery and camp operations
Shop and plant supervision

Sub-sub-accounts (for each main sub-account)

Labour
Supplies
Contract

GENERAL AND ADMINISTRATIVE EXPENSES

Main sub-accounts

Office and warehouse salaries and expense
Communications (telephone, postage, telex, etc.)
Insurance
Security, fire protection and first aid
Personnel
Discounts taken
Workmen's compensation
Unemployment insurance
Vacation pay
Travelling
Bank charges
Project management
Access roads – right of way
Canada pension
Miscellaneous

SURFACE EXPLORATION AND DIAMOND DRILLING

Main sub-accounts

Contract drilling
Geology
Survey
Overhead
Churn drilling
Labour
Supplies
Contract

TECHNICAL ECONOMIC STUDIES

Engineering
Metallurgy
Corporate planning
Facilities engineering
Water study
Orebody evaluation
Townsite study
Land survey programme

Soils engineering evaluation
Seismic study

FEASIBILITY STUDY

Main sub-accounts

Feasibility study by primary contractor
Engineering department re feasibility study
Feasibility study by company
Groundwater – further work
Rock mechanics
Computer consultant
Miscellaneous site engineering and surveys
Townsite study
Geological
Maintain minesite
Land consolidations and option arrangements
Market study
Financing

TABLE A.1

ABC Mining Project sample feasibility cash flow forecast (Project break-even calculation: metal price $1.90/lb)
($000)

Production year	1 $	2 $	3 $	4 $	5 $	6 $	7 $	8 $	9 $	10 $	Totals $
Revenue	10 244	11 284	11 284	11 284	11 284	11 284	11 284	11 284	10 244	5 015	104 491
Operating costs	5 144	5 921	5 727	5 209	5 209	5 209	5 373	5 509	4 966	2 393	50 660
Operating profit	5 100	5 363	5 557	6 075	6 075	6 075	5 911	5 775	5 278	2 622	53 831
Interest (at 9%)	2 713	2 721	2 670	2 525	2 116	1 744	1 401	1 010	669	333	17 902
Profit after interest	2 387	2 642	2 887	3 550	3 959	4 331	4 510	4 765	4 609	2 289	35 929
Taxes											
Mining	62	62	62	62	62	62	67	868	783	63	2 153
Provincial income	—	—	—	—	—	—	—	—	—	—	—
Federal income	—	—	—	—	—	—	—	—	—	—	—
Total taxes	62	62	62	62	62	62	67	868	783	63	2 153
Cash flow	2 325	2 580	2 825	3 488	3 897	4 269	4 443	3 897	3 826	2 226	33 776
Sustaining capital	2 406	2 021	100	100	100	100	100	100	100	(1 498)	3 629
Debt retired	(81)	559	2 725	3 388	3 797	4 169	4 343	3 797	3 726	3 724	30 147
Net cash flow (NCF)	—	—	—	—	—	—	—	—	—	—	—
Present value of NCF (12%)	—	—	—	—	—	—	—	—	—	—	—

TABLE A.2

ABC Mining Project sample feasibility cash flow forecast (Metal price $2.40/lb)
($000)

Production year	1 $	2 $	3 $	4 $	5 $	6 $	7 $	8 $	9 $	10 $	Totals $
Revenue	13 652	15 002	15 002	15 002	15 002	15 002	15 002	15 002	13 652	6 667	138 985
Operating costs	5 144	5 921	5 727	5 209	5 209	5 209	5 373	5 509	4 966	2 393	50 660
Operating profit	8 508	9 081	9 275	9 793	9 793	9 793	9 629	9 493	8 686	4 274	88 325
Interest (at 9%)	2 713	2 414	2 001	1 375	726	56	—	—	—	—	9 285
Profit after interest	5 795	6 667	7 274	8 418	9 067	9 737	9 629	9 493	8 686	4 274	79 040
Taxes											
Mining	62	62	211	1 107	1 215	1 212	1 479	1 607	1 460	365	8 780
Provincial income	—	—			307	766	759	749	685	312	3 578
Federal income	—	—			—	1 848	1 884	1 870	1 716	971	8 289
Total taxes	62	62	211	1 107	1 522	3 826	4 122	4 226	3 861	1 648	20 647
Cash flow	5 733	6 605	7 063	7 311	7 545	5 911	5 507	5 267	4 825	2 626	58 393
Sustaining capital	2 406	2 021	100	100	100	100	100	100	100	(2 053)	3 074
Debt retired	3 327	4 584	6 963	7 211	7 445	617	—	—	—	—	30 147
Net cash flow (NCF)	—	—	—	—	—	5 194	5 407	5 167	4 725	4 679	25 172
Present value of NCF (12%)	—	—	—	—	—	2 223	2 065	1 762	1 436	1 273	8 759

TABLE A.3

ABC Mining Project sample feasibility cash flow forecast (Metal price $2.75/lb)
($000)

Production year	1 $	2 $	3 $	4 $	5 $	6 $	7 $	8 $	9 $	10 $	Totals $
Revenue	16 096	17 669	17 669	17 669	17 669	17 669	17 669	17 669	16 096	7 853	163 728
Operating costs	5 144	5 921	5 727	5 209	5 209	5 209	5 373	5 509	4 966	2 393	50 660
Operating profit	10 952	11 748	11 942	12 460	12 460	12 460	12 296	12 160	11 130	5 460	113 068
Interest (at 9%)	2 713	2 194	1 559	752	—	—	—	—	—	—	7 218
Profit after interest	8 239	9 554	10 383	11 708	12 460	12 460	12 296	12 160	11 130	5 460	105 850
Taxes											
Mining	62	481	1 318	1 640	1 749	1 746	2 012	2 140	1 948	602	13 698
Provincial income	—	—	—	535	982	984	973	963	881	407	5 725
Federal income	—	—	—	453	1 984	2 439	2 697	3 214	2 948	1 316	15 051
Total taxes	62	481	1 318	2 628	4 715	5 169	5 682	6 317	5 777	2 325	34 474
Cash flow	8 177	9 073	9 065	9 080	7 745	7 291	6 614	5 843	5 353	3 135	71 376
Sustaining capital	2 406	2 021	100	100	100	100	100	100	100	(2 053)	3 074
Debt retired	5 771	7 052	8 965	8 359	—	—	—	—	—	—	30 147
Net cash flow (NCF)	—	—	—	621	7 645	7 191	6 514	5 743	5 253	5 188	38 155
Present value of NCF (12%)	—	—	—	333	3 662	3 078	2 488	1 958	1 597	1 411	14 527

TABLE A.4

XYZ Mines Ltd Operations cost summary to July 31, 19-1

Account	Actual ($000) April $	May $	June $	Current month Actual $	Budget $	Variance $	Year to date Actual $	Budget $	Variance $
Operating costs									
10 mine	550	640	720	775 000	804 000	(29 000)	4 925 000	5 004 000	(79 000)
20 Mill	510	480	560	556 000	510 000	46 000	3 874 000	3 709 000	165 000
30 Plant	160	170	170	194 000	218 000	(24 000)	1 096 000	1 043 000	53 000
40 Administration	420	380	400	428 000	434 000	(6 000)	2 795 000	2 812 000	(17 000)
Total operating costs	1 640	1 670	1 850	1 953 000	1 966 000	(13 000)	12 690 000	12 568 000	122 000
Total tons milled	270	220	250	288 000	267 000	21 000	1 733 000	1 660 000	73 000
Cost per ton milled									
10 Mine	2.037	2.909	2.880	2.691	3.011	(0.320)	2.842	3.014	(0.172)
20 Mill	1.889	2.182	2.240	1.931	1.910	0.021	2.235	2.234	0.001
30 Plant	0.593	0.773	0.680	0.674	0.816	(0.142)	0.632	0.628	0.004
40 Administration	1.555	1.727	1.600	1.485	1.626	(0.141)	1.614	1.695	(0.081)
Total cost per ton milled	6.074	7.591	7.400	6.781	7.363	(0.582)	7.323	7.571	(0.248)
Total pounds contained copper	4 100 000	479 000	3 936 000	4 200 000	4 100 000	100 000	25 431 000	29 227 000	(3 796 000)
Cost per pound contained copper									
10 Mine	0.134	0.184	0.183	0.185	0.196	(0.011)	0.194	0.171	0.023
20 Mill	0.124	0.138	0.142	0.132	0.124	0.008	0.152	0.127	0.025
30 Plant	0.039	0.049	0.043	0.046	0.053	(0.007)	0.043	0.036	0.007
40 Administration	0.103	0.109	0.102	0.102	0.107	(0.005)	0.110	0.096	0.014
Total cost per pound contained copper	0.400	0.480	0.470	0.465	0.480	(0.015)	0.499	0.430	0.069

TABLE A.5

XYZ Mines Ltd mill operating cost summary to July 31, 19-1

Actual ($000)			Account	Current month			Year to date		
April $	May $	June $		Actual $	Budget $	Variance $	Actual $	Budget $	Variance $
			Operating costs						
17	16	32	21 Primary crushing	18 190	11 660	6 530	115 000	77 700	37 300
9	9	7	22 Ore stock pile and reclaim	6 630	6 930	(300)	62 400	58 500	3 900
315	276	351	23 Grinding	346 440	337 000	9 440	2 314 600	2 140 100	174 500
121	127	102	24 Flotation	116 770	99 470	17 300	960 100	1 045 800	(85 700)
2	3	5	25 Tailings disposal	(790)	1 950	(2 740)	25 600	18 000	7 600
15	13	17	26 Laboratories	19 310	17 910	1 400	107 000	82 900	24 100
31	36	46	27 Mill general	49 450	35 080	14 370	289 300	286 000	3 300
510	480	560	Total mill operating costs	556 000	510 000	46 000	3 874 000	3 709 000	165 000
270	220	250	Total tons milled	288 000	267 000	21 000	1 733 000	1 660 000	73 000
			Cost per ton milled						
0.063	0.073	0.128	21 Primary crushing	0.063	0.044	0.019	0.066	0.047	0.019
0.033	0.041	0.028	22 Ore stock pile and reclaim	0.023	0.026	(0.003)	0.036	0.035	0.001
1.167	1.255	1.404	23 Grinding	1.203	1.262	(0.059)	1.336	1.289	0.047
0.448	0.577	0.408	24 Flotation	0.405	0.372	0.033	0.554	0.630	(0.076)
0.007	0.014	0.020	25 Tailings disposal	(0.003)	0.007	(0.010)	0.015	0.011	0.004
0.056	0.059	0.068	26 Laboratories	0.067	0.067	0.000	0.062	0.050	0.012
0.115	0.164	0.184	27 Mill general	0.173	0.132	0.041	0.166	0.172	(0.006)
1.889	2.182	2.240	Total mill cost per ton	1.931	1.910	0.021	2.235	2.234	0.001

TABLE A.6

XYZ Mines Ltd cost centre summary–23 grinding to July 31, 19-1

Account	Current month			Year to date		
	Actual $	Budget $	Variance $	Actual $	Budget $	Variance $
Operating costs						
Wages operating	15 750	15 450	300	90 310	92 430	(2 120)
Supplies operating	10		10	16 090	5 000	11 090
Liners	2 350	55 980	(53 630)	390 210	458 180	(67 970)
Balls	136 870	127 460	9 410	727 450	707 210	20 240
	154 980	198 890	(43,910)	1 224 060	1 262 820	(38,760)
Repairs and maintenance						
Wages mechanical	14 790	9 630	5 160	83 960	61 500	22 460
Wages electrical	3 220	2 590	630	24 640	16 560	8 080
Supplies mechanical	50 410	16 230	34 180	246 370	116 550	129 820
Supplies electrical	670	4 300	(3 630)	3 830	14 560	(10 730)
	69 090	32 750	36 340	358 800	209 170	149 630
Services internal						
Power	122 370	105 360	17 010	731 740	668 110	63 630
Cost centre total	346 440	337 000	9 440	2 314 600	2 140 100	174 500

TABLE A.7
XYZ Mines Ltd cost centre detail–23 grinding to July 31, 19-1

Account	Name	Month $	Year to date $
2300	Grinding (general)		
103	Wages operating	15 750	90 310
105	Supplies operating	10	16 090
201	Wages mechanical	3 400	7 560
211	Wages electrical	1 450	4 440
215	Supplies mechanical	3 280	17 250
216	Supplies electrical	70	920
510	Power	122 370	731 740
		146 330	868 310
2301	Ball mill		
141	Liners		101 450
142	Balls	39 560	238 390
201	Wages mechanical	1 120	12 890
211	Wages electrical	230	2 970
215	Supplies mechanical	3 440	10 060
216	Supplies electrical	70	560
		44 420	366 320
2302	Semi-autogenous mill		
141	Liners	2 350	288 760
142	Balls	97 310	489 060
201	Wages mechanical	9 490	50 470
211	Wages electrical	1 540	17 130
215	Supplies mechanical	37 390	159 060
216	Supplies electrical	530	2 090
		148 610	1 006 570
2303	Pumps		
201	Wages mechanical	780	13 040
211	Wages electrical		100
215	Supplies mechanical	6 300	60 000
216	Supplies electrical		260
		7 080	73 400
	Cost centre total	346 440	2 314 600

Index

The main headings of this index list the chronological stages involved in setting up an operational mine as Search, Acquisition, Exploration, Evaluation, Feasibility studies, Development and construction, Production.